Praise for *Against the Grain*

Welcome to Ecclesiastes—one of the most crabby, irksome, beautiful, and challenging books in all of scripture. Wander through Ecclesiastes with Ray Waddle as your guide, and you'll discover buried treasure, stunning insight, and spiritual gifts at every turn in the journey.

—WILLIAM H. WILLIMON
Bishop, Birmingham Episcopal Area,
The United Methodist Church
Author of *Remember Who You Are* and *Sunday Dinner*

Ecclesiastes is the most unusual and enigmatic author in the Bible. The result of Ray Waddle's musings on the thoughts of this lovable curmudgeon is a book that is both profound and entertaining.

—JOHN MCQUISTON
Author of *Always We Begin Again* and
A Prayer Book for the Twenty-first Century

AGAINST THE GRAIN

Unconventional Wisdom
from Ecclesiastes

RAY WADDLE

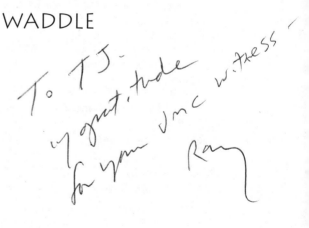

To TJ.
in gratitude
for your UMC witness

Ray

UPPER
ROOM BOOKS®
NASHVILLE

AGAINST THE GRAIN: Unconventional Wisdom from Ecclesiastes
Copyright © 2005 by Ray Waddle
All rights reserved.

The Upper Room Web site: www.upperroom.org

At the time of publication, all Web sites referenced in this book were valid. However, due to the fluid nature of the Internet some addresses may have changed or the content may no longer be relevant.

An extension of the copyright page appears on page 160.

Cover design: LeftCoast Design
Cover photo: Martin Baurraud / Gettyimages.com
Interior design: Nancy Terzian / nterdesign.com
First printing: 2005

Library of Congress Cataloging-in-Publication Data
Waddle, Ray, 1956–
    Against the grain : unconventional wisdom from Ecclesiastes / Ray Waddle.
        p. cm.
    ISBN 0-8358-9813-X
    1. Bible. O. T. Ecclesiastes—Meditations. I. Title.
    BS1475.54.W33 2005
    223'.806—dc22
                                                          2004030831

Printed in the United States of America

To my mother
and the memory
of my father

CONTENTS

Prologue	Feel the Wind	9
Introduction	Ecclesiastes and Us	13
Chapter 1	Minority Report	19
Chapter 2	Blues Memoir	35
Chapter 3	Anthem of the World	51
Chapter 4	Rich and Famous	63
Chapter 5	"Let Your Words Be Few"	75
Chapter 6	Interlude: Hide-and-Seek	87
Chapter 7	Mourning Glory	95
Chapter 8	Wise Guy	107
Chapter 9	God's Fingerprints	117
Chapter 10	Election Day	127
Chapter 11	Who Knows?	137
Chapter 12	God Alone	145
Epilogue	Ecclesiastes and Christ	155
Notes		157
About the Author		159

ACKNOWLEDGMENTS

I owe thanks to all the people whose eyes light up
at the name of Ecclesiastes because they discovered
him on their own, like buried treasure.

Thanks also to the scholars I cite in this book
and to all who face the adventure of
reading Ecclesiastes in every generation.

Finally, my loving gratitude goes to Lisa,
who makes dreams come true.

CONTENTS

Prologue	Feel the Wind	9
Introduction	Ecclesiastes and Us	13
Chapter 1	Minority Report	19
Chapter 2	Blues Memoir	35
Chapter 3	Anthem of the World	51
Chapter 4	Rich and Famous	63
Chapter 5	"Let Your Words Be Few"	75
Chapter 6	Interlude: Hide-and-Seek	87
Chapter 7	Mourning Glory	95
Chapter 8	Wise Guy	107
Chapter 9	God's Fingerprints	117
Chapter 10	Election Day	127
Chapter 11	Who Knows?	137
Chapter 12	God Alone	145
Epilogue	Ecclesiastes and Christ	155
Notes		157
About the Author		159

ACKNOWLEDGMENTS

I owe thanks to all the people whose eyes light up
at the name of Ecclesiastes because they discovered
him on their own, like buried treasure.

Thanks also to the scholars I cite in this book
and to all who face the adventure of
reading Ecclesiastes in every generation.

Finally, my loving gratitude goes to Lisa,
who makes dreams come true.

PROLOGUE
FEEL THE WIND

This is a book about finding God in the strangest corner of the Bible—
the book of Ecclesiastes—and why it's ignored and what if it weren't.

After September 11, 2001, two questions haunt us: Are we safe?
and Is God on our side? The issue of God today invades our politics, dreams, and entertainments. This book addresses some common assumptions about God and how Ecclesiastes illuminates
them. Or contradicts them. Or points the way to a place of uncom-
mon serenity and wisdom, all gifts of God.

Ecclesiastes is located close to the middle of the Holy Bible
itself, in the Hebrew Scriptures, or Old Testament, set between the
books of Proverbs and Song of Solomon. Yet this book is usually
ignored by organized religion. The author is a moody, enigmatic
fellow. Pastors pass over him because he lacks the news of resurrection. Rabbis turn away because his startling outbursts look like a
mess of contradiction. He's considered too disturbing, too pes-
simistic, for the official version of American spirituality.

But Ecclesiastes is something rare: a poet of emotional honesty
and spiritual realism. At first his words are hard to bear. We're
accustomed to a different style. Public religion today arrives fast
and furious, holy news wrapped in exciting, upbeat production values. People are dazzled, breathless, eager to join, no time for questions. But at the end of the day, the world is still confused, fearful,
dissatisfied, angry, violent, forgetful.

Ecclesiastes offers a counterinvitation. Like an ancient stranger riding into town, he comes with candor and courage. He challenges a twenty-first-century idolatry—the careless use of God's name to bless every self-serving political and religious purpose. Ecclesiastes stands as a rebuke to this breaking of the third commandment, the widespread taking of God's name in vain, whether to justify political agendas, spiritual hypocrisy, or murderous terrorism.

So this is a book about the neglected themes of Ecclesiastes: the goodness of creation; the fingerprints of providence; the frustrations of spirit in a world of affluence and suffering; the beauty of everyday pleasures; the duty to remember the dead; the duty, indeed, to be happy. It's about feeling the wind in your face, the wind of being alive. Despite his reputation, Ecclesiastes marks the surprising arrival of consolation and hope.

You'll find the entire book of Ecclesiastes enclosed in this book, a little at a time, and one reader's attempt at a conversation with it. I wrote this book for three reasons: (1) I'm a writer intrigued by how public religion has neglected Ecclesiastes; (2) I'm a church-goer who wants to take the whole Bible seriously; (3) I'm a professional observer of the religion scene who thinks Ecclesiastes offers an antidote to the world's abuses of politicized religion and the deadly use of belief to promote terror, suffering, and injustice.

As a Christian I don't believe Ecclesiastes gets the last word. He doesn't have the whole story. Yet we can't avoid this troublesome, against-the-grain voice from scripture. Christians keep a strange relationship to the Old Testament: we conveniently quote what we like and shun what we don't. But believers should read Ecclesiastes—with alertness, not fear. He teaches and toughens. He tells of the ways of God in a hard world. His writing contains moods of the spiritual life—moods of God—that never get publicized in the highly competitive marketplace of religion. He presses readers to work harder to find a balance between praise and remembrance— praise of eternal God and remembrance of everyday suffering—all at once. He's in the Bible for a reason.

To encounter Ecclesiastes is to argue with him or embrace him but always to feel his shadow across our jittery new century. He arrives just in time, every time.

❧

It is the glory of God to conceal things, but the glory of kings is to search things out.

—Proverbs 25:2

❧

[God] has planted eternity in the human heart, but even so, people cannot see the whole scope of God's work from beginning to end.

—Ecclesiastes 3:11, NLT

❧

All scripture is inspired by God and is useful for teaching, for reproof, for correction, and for training in righteousness, so that everyone who belongs to God may be proficient, equipped for every good work.

—2 Timothy 3:16-17

INTRODUCTION
ECCLESIASTES AND US

I was still a teenager when I first encountered Ecclesiastes. I never got over the shock.

It arrived as a quote at the beginning of a Hemingway novel, *The Sun Also Rises,* a story of disillusioned wanderers in post–World War I Europe. It's Hemingway's best book.

But the quote stopped me cold. It sounded exhausted, discouraged—the way a real person actually feels sometimes. As a church-going teenager, I was flabbergasted. Here was a statement in holy scripture announcing the opposite of Sunday school uplift. It read:

> One generation passeth away, and another generation cometh: but the earth abideth for ever. The sun also ariseth, and the sun goeth down, and hasteth to his place where he arose. The wind goeth toward the south, and turneth about unto the north; it whirleth about continually, and the wind returneth again according to his circuits. All the rivers run into the sea; yet the sea is not full; unto the place from whence the rivers come, thither they return again. (Eccles. 1:4-7, KJV)

This was the Bible? No one had ever told me about Ecclesiastes. I had not heard this in church. In the South where I grew up, people cited scripture publicly all the time, yet they never quoted Ecclesiastes.

As I discovered, this is how many people learn of Ecclesiastes in the first place—not from Sunday morning worship time or the press releases of robed denominational leaders but from the larger, noisy world of pop culture. If you're a baby boomer, chances are you first got wind of Ecclesiastes from the Byrds' "Turn, Turn, Turn," which was a number-one hit in 1965 and quotes from Ecclesiastes' third chapter ("There is a season . . . and a time to every purpose under heaven. . . . A time to build up, a time to break down; a time to dance, a time to mourn"). The lyrics are the oldest ever used in a Top 40 tune.

Quoted in a popular college novel like *The Sun Also Rises*, Ecclesiastes surfaces as an unauthorized delegate of biblical religion wandering outside the sanctuary and into the big world of late-night cafés and difficult human relations, a tough Hemingwayish place where pious jargon doesn't get far. Here, a sacred biblical author was being quoted without institutional spin. He was leaving his own trail of plainspoken truth telling.

Soon I decided I'd better turn to the book of Ecclesiastes on my own. The revelations continued. This biblical testimony departed from a thousand soothing church devotional lessons I'd heard. Ecclesiastes offered something unusual—spiritual realism. He posed a dissent from the official message that God's will and purposes are always clear. He said things like:

All is vanity! . . . All things are wearisome; more than one can express. . . . There is nothing new under the sun. (1:2, 8, 9)

There is nothing better for mortals than to eat and drink,
and find enjoyment in their toil. (2:24)

God is in heaven, and you upon earth;
therefore let your words be few. (5:2)

The experience of reading Ecclesiastes was jarring and disturbing. It was also liberating.

My college-age discovery of Ecclesiastes, a renegade sacred point of view situated in the middle of the Holy Bible, took place nearly thirty years ago. Despite decades of churchgoing since then, I've never heard a sermon about Ecclesiastes.

There's an official nervousness whenever Ecclesiastes is in the neighborhood. And no wonder. Ecclesiastes is the oddest book in the Bible, perhaps the strangest sacred writing in the history of religion. Its spirit defies the rest of scripture. It has a skeptical bent. At times it is recklessly harsh and despairing. The writer, called Ecclesiastes, or the Preacher, or the Teacher, or Qoheleth, or Koheleth, doesn't talk about the history of Israel or God's mighty acts in human affairs, like most other books of scripture do. He reports instead on his own experience of spiritual matters. Ecclesiastes is disillusioned by human ambition, the seductions of material things, and he doesn't hide his feelings.

The spirit of Ecclesiastes is foreign to any simple expectation of divine daily arrival, and that puts him at odds with virtually every impulse of the religious scene today. He's doubtful of the human capacity to grasp the will of God. In the book of Ecclesiastes, God the Creator is mysterious indeed: God passes out no party favors. God bides God's time.

Yet Ecclesiastes' message is not a meltdown of pessimism. He refuses to drain the earth of spiritual consequence. He believes God exists. God is sovereign, in control. Wisdom and common sense both urge one human response: reverence. We should feel awe for this Creator. Yet we are not privy to the divine master plan. So Ecclesiastes writes, "There is nothing better for mortals than to eat and drink, and find enjoyment in their toil. This also, I saw, is from the hand of God" (2:24). God invites people to live this life fully, gratefully. That's God's gift. In return we have a duty to be happy.

Ecclesiastes is an unusual ambassador of the religious life. He brings news of faith observed and felt at street level. He's a realist in the real world: he describes spiritual moods that manage to sneak up on a person on slow weekday afternoons, lonely evenings, or long stretches of ordinary time—when "All is vanity" sounds plausible, and God's relation to the world might well seem unknowable. Ecclesiastes chronicles such moments.

He's hip-deep in paradoxes and turmoil himself. He resists any claim to knowing the will of God, yet he's also filled with awe of

God. He's skeptical about the human grasp of truth yet upholds belief in the sovereignty of the Lord. He sags with spiritual weariness yet burns with a passion for divine wisdom.

This "Preacher" does not claim to be a credentialed clergyperson or prophet. He's something unpredictable—a lay philosopher, going his own way. But he holds to a baseline of faith and ethics, underwritten by the Almighty. His message might be boiled down this way:

- Everything passes away.
- God knows all, judges all.
- Keep God's commandments.
- Enjoy the world.

Our times are not for the faint of heart. Nor is Ecclesiastes. He lodges a protest against the religious and cultural establishment of his day. More than two thousand years later, nothing has changed. He still goes against the national grain. He's not part of the national conversation, whatever the nation.

We might dismiss Ecclesiastes as a crank, except for one inconvenient fact: somehow he has a book of his own in the Bible. His words come with the aura of divine biblical authority. His words, not ours, are found in holy scripture.

After reading my Hemingway and finishing college and then graduate school, I became a journalist, namely a religion editor for a big morning newspaper. My assignment was to cover the busy world of contemporary religion and spirituality in America and beyond—doctrinal debates, Bible sales, street prophets, Pentecostal miracles, atheistic protests, Christian music celebrities, seminary dramas, papal decrees, worship innovations, stadium prayers, spirit-filled inspirations, frauds, and mysteries.

It's a dazzling, clashing scene—a society awash in divine claims, good deeds, competitive truths, mountaintop pursuits, saintly visions, fist-pumping certitudes, hotheaded discontent. Driving the faith of millions is a rock-bottom conviction that God, the inconceivable Creator of universe and eternity, has intimate regard and sway over every decision we make every day, no matter how trivial.

After nearly twenty years on the religion beat, I decided to quit the job and step away from the sanctified headlines. I needed to hear myself think again. My new wanderings led me to an old, forgotten address: Ecclesiastes. And there I knocked.

I turned to this overlooked book as an experiment. A paradox fascinated me: believers of the Bible act as if this very book from scripture doesn't exist. It goes unmentioned. That's understandable. It's disorienting to think the God-inspired Bible includes a voice of such withering skepticism. But can we ignore this sacred author? Can he coexist with the sunny church marquee sentiments of faith today? What if Ecclesiastes were let loose in sacred assemblies and denominational meetings? How should today's Christian read Ecclesiastes? There are intriguing points of contact between Ecclesiastes and Jesus. Jesus warned against confident predictions of God's future judgment. So did Ecclesiastes. Jesus urged people to cast off worries and seek God's rule today. So did Ecclesiastes, in his own way. Did Jesus know about Ecclesiastes, who lived perhaps 250 years before him? We'll take up these questions.

With the 9/11 darkness of terrorism and war came a new, terrible opening on the wisdom of Ecclesiastes. A season of spiritual fear and emptiness, security anxiety, dread of abysmal mass destruction, no sense that the horror will end, the secret worry that our faith and institutions cannot match these shadowy TV slaughters—such thoughts suddenly drove people back to scripture for answers, back to the Gospels, the Psalms, the Prophets.

Ecclesiastes waits there too. His presence proclaims that even spiritual weariness and discouragement, along with the promise of divine truth, have their legitimate moment in God's world. Ecclesiastes is there as a kind of memoirist, rare in the history of scripture, offering a personal report of spiritual false starts and inspired breakthroughs, a humane biblical voice against the bristling juggernaut of religious violence that is shaping the twenty-first century. He offers an antidote to overheated analysis and creedal controversy, things that lead to religious division, name-calling, even killing.

Through it all, he brings news—our duty to be happy.

Turning to Ecclesiastes, I was looking for something personal too—a little clarity, a way to behold God and be beholden to God in the real world of awful contradictions: a world full of music and disaster, wildflowers and starvation, tenderness and mental illness, including the mental illness of loved ones in my own life.

Everything comes down to a few big questions: How should we spend this waking life? How does God relate to us? What should be our response? Why do injustices flourish? Is the Bible true? Does God exist? Where is God?

Old Ecclesiastes raises the oldest questions of the spiritual search: Can we figure out our needs, our salvation, on our own, or do we need outside revelation to complete the picture? Can our own hearts and minds be our guide, or are they incomplete, faulty, untrustworthy, incapable of leading us to happiness?

Ecclesiastes won't let up with his questions and his findings. He does something else too. He refuses to forget the dead and the suffering. His words carry respectful memories of the suffering of all who have passed to the other side, forgotten by history. He is their commemorator. The task he lays before us is to believe in God, relate to God, speak of God, while at the same moment remembering the dead, the oppressed, the frightening fragility of life, the sudden unexplainable ways of death. To claim God's favor in our daily lives and agendas, even for every trivial lucky break and game-winning field goal, without acknowledging the world of suffering, the world of other people's struggles, is to use God's name in vain.

In the end, as Ecclesiastes confides, experience is the teacher—earthly experience, often in the dark, the future unknown, but God frames the whole picture nonetheless. Ecclesiastes warns of the folly of vain strivings. Our busy culture of fast-track careerism, abundance, and insomnia always provides Ecclesiastes with new material, new chapters all but written. Our moment in the sun is richer, less cluttered and anxious, for having Ecclesiastes' strange, irksome witness nearby.

CHAPTER 1
MINORITY REPORT

The words of the Teacher, the son of David, king in Jerusalem.
—Ecclesiastes 1:1

Yesterday on a busy street I saw a church marquee. The sign read, "With God's love and guidance, I welcome the new year." As these signs go, the message was humble and hopeful, not as flashy as others I've noticed lately, like:

- Dusty Bibles lead to dirty lives.
- A miracle is something extraordinary with no strings attached.
- Pray for a good harvest, but continue to hoe.
- How will you spend eternity—smoking or nonsmoking?
- Free trip to heaven—details inside!

But there it was: "With God's love and guidance, I welcome the new year." It's a generous thought. It assumes the best, an ease of divine access, the to and fro between here and heaven, a connection to the divine energies. It's made despite the world's deep sea of suffering. It defies the gravity of bad news.

This particular morning's headlines were awful—blood and anger in Iraq and Israel, financial swindles on Wall Street, fears of epidemics, rumors of terrorism. Maybe that's why I pulled over and wrote it down, this benign snippet of holy intention. I could feel the wind behind the words. Maybe it gave a clue to something.

Every day the dazzling marketplace of religion surrounds us with messages about who we are and Who's behind it all. Announcements of the sacred compete for our attention by the million— church signs, toll-free numbers, celebrity workshops, annual assemblies, revival hymns, scholarly arguments, denominational initiatives, banquet prayers, books of truth, tears of joy.

The religious marketplace provides a daily index of energy and ingenuity—a humming dynamo open at all hours, with room for every sort of competitor of faith to succeed.

It's a scene of fascination and inspiration.

Also of chaos and menace.

On the one hand, religious practice creates humane goodwill, gentleness, and charity. Every day, people whisper valentines to heaven, prayers thousands of years old, in order to find healing and wholeness. They carry forward the long adventure of monotheism, with patient trust in the universe, and disciplines of faithfulness, truth telling, and compassion.

Turn a little to one side, and the angle is different. We live in a teeming, dangerous era of conflicting public claims of faith, culture wars, religious wars, suicide bombings—all in God's name. There's a mad clamor for the divine, a jockeying for prestige and power. Armed certitudes plague the world, fueled by angry arrogance, self-pity, fantasies of doctrinal purity, and apocalypse. Ethics, hospitality, the Golden Rule, and good manners are shouted down, blown to bits. An awkward contradiction defines the times. A rising sophistication, borne on waves of high-tech prosperity and far-flung travel, runs neck and neck with florid paranoias, medieval grievances, and red-hot hatreds of the stranger. Religious justification laces through it all. Critics rise from their seats in a chorus of disgust. Writer Martin Amis recently blurted, "Since it is no longer permissible to disparage any single faith or creed, let us start disparaging all of them."

At the moment, though, someone else has the floor.

Stop a minute and listen. Maybe it's nighttime or thereabouts as you read this. Ecclesiastes is that sort of subject. He comes from a nighttime place, when things get quiet and you can hear thoughts that are strictly your own. In the after-hours depths, away from the deadlines and pat answers, it's possible to feel the mystery of life's flow, the unsettled ground of life yet to live.

Ecclesiastes stands ready to make a cameo appearance, but only after the big-time religious marketplace has folded up its billowing tents and vanished for the night. The daily ever-renewing spiritual expo never manages to reserve a booth for Ecclesiastes and his sunset moods.

Tonight the rules change. It is Ecclesiastes who speaks—not the best-selling conference keynoters, the gurus, or the Web site nihilists.

Ecclesiastes—also called the Teacher, or the Preacher, or the Speaker, or "Qoheleth" or "Koheleth"—announces himself out of the blue, from an unlit corner in the sacred text, coming right after the book of Proverbs with its elegant compendium of cautious wisdom and piety, and just before the sweet passions of the Song of Solomon.

Ecclesiastes' identity, so forcefully declared in this first verse, is a mystery. Who is he? Son of King David, he says. Centuries of tradition, Jewish and Christian, identified the author as Solomon, one of David's sons. Solomon, the Old Testament monarch, builder, and administrator, succeeded David as king of Israel, reigning with supreme grandeur for forty years until his death around 930 BCE. He was famously wise; perhaps he wrote the book of Ecclesiastes in a weary mood of impatient candor. An ancient quip says King Solomon wrote the book of Song of Solomon in his youth, the book of Proverbs in mature years, and Ecclesiastes in his bitter old age.

Yet the name Solomon never actually appears in the book of Ecclesiastes. And for more than a hundred years now, the main centers of biblical scholarship have rejected the ancient notion that Solomon wrote Ecclesiastes. They say the book was probably written many centuries later, perhaps no earlier than 250 BCE, by an unnamed Jewish philosopher or by his students after his death, reconstructing their notes from his open-air lectures.

Whoever Ecclesiastes was, someone very old who sounds very new crashes in. Stop and listen. It's a sound coming from outside the regulated courts of the religious scene, a lone individual speaking to a sea of souls:

࿇

Vanity of vanities, says the Teacher,
vanity of vanities! All is vanity. (1:2)

And he says impossible things. "All is vanity"—the most startling sentence in the Bible. To the organizers of normal public uplift, it's alarming indeed. It flies against everything we're taught. These are not words for greeting the morning. The statement reads like defeatism. How could it be in the Bible?

The prestige of Solomon made it possible. The old association with Solomon's name gave the book of Ecclesiastes enough holiness and clout to win the day when the rabbis debated which books to place in the Hebrew Bible. The decision took time. The Torah (the first five books) were established and accepted probably between 550 and 300 BCE, and the books of the Prophets by the time of the first century CE.[1] The rest of the Old Testament, a block called the Writings, which includes Ecclesiastes, was not settled until sometime after 70 CE, after the Romans' destruction of Jerusalem.

"All is vanity." Scholars zero in on the meanings of *vanity*. In modern usage the word usually means egotism and self-absorption. But the Hebrew word for vanity, *hebel*, is closer to vapor, wind, breath, something ephemeral and wispy, insubstantial, gone in a moment. Ecclesiastes is champion of the word, its stoutest biblical defender: *vanity* occurs thirty-eight times in the book of Ecclesiastes, more than anywhere else in the Old Testament, where it's found seventy-three times.

"All is vanity." It sounds like a suicide note. The meaninglessness of it all, etc. And yet . . . the fact that he taught these words, hoping to convey insight to others, shows he cared more than he let on. If all is vanity, then why bother to teach others? Why even write the book of Ecclesiastes? The fact that Ecclesiastes is in the Bible at all means that his message is not one of meaninglessness. It's there as a burst of rough wisdom—an entry point, oddly enough, on a journey that leads to peace of mind.

It's the first of many paradoxes about Ecclesiastes. He arrives to say: Life passes; nothing is permanent; we can't know the full meaning of it all—yet we will press on. It's what God wants of us. Ecclesiastes is commonly dismissed as the great pessimist of scripture. The charge is unconvincing. Ecclesiastes does not turn away from an argument—a relationship—with eternity. Life is plagued by contradiction, inconsistency. We carry on despite that predicament. So does belief. So does Ecclesiastes.

What do people gain from all the toil
at which they toil under the sun?
A generation goes, and a generation comes,
but the earth remains forever. (1:3-4)

I'm using the New Revised Standard Version (NRSV) of the Bible to supply Ecclesiastes' words in this book. The NRSV, accurate and current, still carries vestiges of poetic phrasing from the days of the King James Version, four hundred years old. At the moment, though, I miss the King James, where verse 3 says: "What profit hath a man of all his labour which he taketh under the sun?"

It's unfortunate the word *profit* doesn't survive current translations, which prefer more casual expressions. *Profit* packs a history of rebuke in its two short syllables. The word resounds with sharp echoes from Old Testament to New, where Jesus asks his own searching question: "For what will it profit them to gain the whole world and forfeit their life?" (Mark 8:36).

Profit catches our eye. It's a deadly serious word now; it's on everyone's mind. Profit margins . . . profit shares . . . *profit* dominates the day job, the media coverage, the conversation. It makes or breaks the American way of life. Workplace anxiety, job cuts, massive CEO salaries, and fraudulent accounting practices are the pressure marks of the new standard, the big bottom line, the scream for more profits. Everything flows from there: a faster pace, more productivity, more cell phone numbers to learn, more mortgage options, more Web sites, more memos, more loopholes, more sleepless nights. It leaves people (me) sometimes wondering in the dark, *What's the point? Why am I here?*—and trying to sort out a credible answer.

Ecclesiastes, a loner unconcerned with delicate diplomacy and rhetoric, does not varnish his words: why labor at all, if death wins in the end? The question sounds too harsh for mass consumption. But Ecclesiastes urges readers to look at the biggest possible picture, God's picture, in order to face the fact of mortality and the question of what should one do with this life.

Ecclesiastes' question in this passage hangs there, staring. It travels through the centuries, ending at every doorstep.

The sun rises and the sun goes down,
and hurries to the place where it rises.
The wind blows to the south, and goes around to the north;
round and round goes the wind,
and on its circuits the wind returns. (1:5-6)

When I go to Kansas, I think of Ecclesiastes.

I go to visit relatives and feel that stiff wind in my face. Other people drive across the "featureless" Great Plains as fast as they can, on the way to somewhere else. To me the region is a revelation to linger over. On the High Plains of America, the wind is a constant force, an ancient music. It mocks human history and designs. It's a kind of geographical book of Ecclesiastes.

My mother grew up here, on a family farm in western Kansas, Trego County, during the Dust Bowl of the 1930s. You can still see grassy slopes along barns and fences, former dust dunes from those hard times.

The Dust Bowl, the Dirty Thirties, was an epic disaster, almost biblical in severity. The dust came in tall, angry clouds and piled up inches thick even in the house. You couldn't keep it out. Rain stayed away for years. Fields blew away. Seed disappeared. Livestock suffocated and perished. Foreclosures flourished. Many people got out, walked away, and headed to California on the mere rumor of decent work. My mother's family hung on until the rains returned by the end of the decade.

By the late 1940s my mother moved on, marrying my Arkansas-bred father and settling way South, where I was Louisiana-born and raised. But we annually made the long road trip to rural Kansas to visit uncles, aunts, cousins. Never had I seen such a sky. It carried a theology new to me: the awe of creation, stark, bigger than my thoughts, relentlessly silent, nonnegotiable. In the city, talk of God is gregarious, intimate, easy. In so many city churches, God is characterized as accessible, friendly, human scale. Under the Western sky, the scale of nature is vast, sometimes inhospitable. Farmers must depend on the weather—a force obviously beyond their control—for miracles of harvest. Here you are forced to admit: life is short; the questions are many; and this sky and wind, God's creation itself, will outlast us all.

Prayers on the plains sound different from those in the city. I've heard them in little white wooden churches off the back roads. You hear prayers for seasonable weather, a fair price for crops, prayers for the survival of small communities and family farms. Running through them all is a tone of hard-won humility. People here know humanity is small on the horizon; so much is out of our hands. Killer tornadoes and ruinous hail arrive from the same sky that brings healing sunshine and gentle rains.

In the 1930s the prayers were especially desperate, even as the rest of the nation was spared this sort of reckoning, the trauma of choking dust and drought of God's Great Plains. Since then, the plains's agricultural drama of suffering for the land has been largely ignored, left out of the larger American religious narrative. The cheerful prosperity of the twenty-first-century marketplace of religion leaves big stretches of difficult reality undigested.

Dust Bowl, drought, infant mortality, financial uncertainty—all inevitably complicate one's understanding of God. They shyly pose a different set of religious values that the mainstream nervously neglects—humility, stoicism, silence, gratitude, the spirituality of suffering. They count more than complicated doctrine. They matter to my Methodist churchgoing mother, who, still in Louisiana and decades removed from the Kansas Dust Bowl, regards every sunny day as a blessing to behold.

Next time you're driving across the Great Plains, stop along the road, listen to the roaring wind, and take out your handy copy of Ecclesiastes. In western Kansas and every place like it, the spirit of Ecclesiastes rides on the incessant wind with a story to tell.

All streams run to the sea, but the sea is not full;
to the place where the streams flow,
there they continue to flow. (1:7)

So far, Ecclesiastes hasn't even mentioned God. The Preacher's gaze is horizontal, not vertical. He is preoccupied with what he can observe and experience of earth. He veers away from organized religion's custom of telling the stories of God's mighty acts in history and everyday life while ignoring the natural world itself.

But the book of Genesis says God made it all and deemed it good: "God called the dry land Earth, and the waters that were gathered together he called Seas. And God saw that it was good" (Gen. 1:10). Genesis seems to weigh heavily on Ecclesiastes' mind. In this brief passage the sea is his subject, the font of created life, the biggest thing on earth there is to see.

The sea triggers big, uncontrollable thoughts of birth, mortality, heaven, and oblivion all at once. The seaside is a place where anxieties empty if the beach isn't too crowded and there's plenty of sunscreen. Stresses ooze away. The body's own elements join chorus with the basic units of sand, salt, wind, water, sun. The challenges of daily life—the career worries, the bills due, the rattles under the hood—dissolve away in the crashing seascape. At such moments of beach vacation bliss, it feels like a homecoming to stare out at sea.

Then Ecclesiastes notes, "but the sea is not full." A little shoot of sadness runs up my spine. The sea's project isn't completed. Life is finite and unpredictable, my desires never ending, never completely fulfilled. I can feel incompleteness in the drama of family, career, vocation. The deaths of loved ones mount. It's a project never rounded to a tidy finish, this sea of conscious life—nearly infinite, blurring at the edges, a wonder to behold, never full, never fully understood.

*All things are wearisome; more than one can express;
the eye is not satisfied with seeing,
or the ear filled with hearing. (1:8)*

The other night I watched the Super Bowl. I looked forward to it, as always. I'm a football fan from the ancient days of Bart Starr and Jim Brown, so I enjoy the annual inflation of this NFL showdown into a midwinter carnival, a celebration of excess to get us all through a late-January Sunday night. It's like one last shout after the glittering festivities of December, before the shadow of Lent starts to creep across the calendar. It's America's biggest party.

By halftime, the spirit of Ecclesiastes made an unexpected visit; feelings "full of weariness" snuck into the room as the night wore on. The frantic halftime entertainment was lip-synched without apology. The rock-and-roll celebrity salute to the dead of 9/11 was too much. The eye indeed was not satisfied with seeing. But I did my consumer best, sitting on the couch for five hours, eating the whole bag of corn chips before the third quarter, enjoying the clever commercials every ten minutes.

An old restlessness set in, I admit—a sullenness, the blahs. Everyone knows the feeling after watching television half the night. This fatigue, this washed-out TV numbness, is a daily national fact. It is never discussed publicly. Certainly no one in prime-time ever addresses this essence of exhaustion. It's never on the cover of *Newsweek* or featured on public radio. Yet the sullenness is an old story, the oldest on earth. It drives many a spiritual search: I am bored almost immediately by the things I crave and accumulate. It's why the Bible got written in the first place, the story of sin and redemption, the original restlessness and its solution.

Weariness, exhaustion—spiritual facts of life. Here Ecclesiastes reported it long before televised sports extravaganzas, when the world was a very unplugged place. What he delivers is memorable news indeed—the most publicly extravagant utterance of exhaustion in the history of the world.

᠅

What has been is what will be,
and what has been done is what will be done;
there is nothing new under the sun.
Is there a thing of which it is said, "See, this is new"?
It has already been, in the ages before us. (1:9-10)

Assume, if you will, that Ecclesiastes lived in Jerusalem in 250 BCE. All sorts of things were happening. Several decades before, Alexander the Great had conquered the Holy Land. The First Punic War was underway between Rome and Carthage. The Colossus of Rhodes, one of the Seven Wonders of the Ancient World, had been completed some thirty years before. Ecclesiastes' region of the world was moving deeply into the shadow of Greek political power and cultural dominance, something new in the land of the Bible.

Still, even twenty-three hundred years ago, the world already felt old, used up, and depleted of excitement, as Ecclesiastes gives witness. "What has been is what will be."

Ecclesiastes' mood rudely challenges a modern religious attitude that gets so much press these days—the apocalyptic vision waiting for Something Big to happen. Movies, books, and radio preachers feed the expectation of the big biblical blowout. Best-selling novels tap into imaginations honed for the end time. Connoisseurs of Armageddon scan the skies and the headlines for signs of the times and clairvoyant signals of the not-yet. They envision the fiery obliteration of the present, an ultimate purification, an escape from the burdensome details of the now, the heavy tasks of relationships, democracy, religious faith itself.

Ecclesiastes believes in the future judgment of God too, but he declines to fantasize the details. He remains skeptical of the human capacity to know the divine plan or get it right.

There's nothing new under the sun, he famously says. He will not be bamboozled by the demands of the new and improved, the latest pop diva, the latest doomsday scenario. The new is a rehash of the old. Ecclesiastes seems comforted by that. The world is not collapsing. There is grief; there is awful dread; but the old sun also rises.

The people of long ago are not remembered,
nor will there be any remembrance
of people yet to come
by those who come after them. (1:11)

For nearly two decades I wrote religion stories for the newspaper, between two and three hundred a year, hoping to add something to the memory bank of our day—to tell people's stories, report events that define America, get closer to the mysteries of faith—and defy oblivion, the tide of forgetfulness.

Over time I noticed certain stories kept resurfacing—spiritual trends that would flare up, die down, be forgotten, then somehow resurrect a few years later, refurbished as new revelation. End-of-the-world scares, for instance, erupted in the mid-1980s. Some Bible-reading believers quit their jobs and waited for the end. They said good-bye to their friends. They even euthanized their beloved pets. It was a time of communal hysteria and Bible misreading. Then nothing happened; the end was postponed again. Their discredited leaders waited a few years, then retooled their dark predictions, confident that people had forgotten the millennial fevers of the 1980s and now were ready for more.

More benignly, angel sightings were big in the early '90s. People credited the work of angels for rescuing them from winter storms, or an angelic tap on the shoulder for averting car crashes. The stories eventually went underground. The media moved on. Then came the millennium, and daily journalism gave angel stories yet another revival.

I felt complicit in this endless cycle of amnesia and revision, the incessant stimulation of the public, the lack of perspective on the past.

Ecclesiastes groans under the sheer wastes of historical time, the recycling of history, the endless passing of generations. Thinking about the fading canvas of human memory keeps him up at night.

At the turn of the millennium, a preacher on cable TV assured us Jesus would return next week. Was it true? An acquaintance who believed it urged me to write the story. Declare the news, she said. Sound the warning. This could finally be it—Armageddon next

Thursday. But I had written my fill of such stories. They had become an embarrassment, a cheapening of God and God's future designs, a vain use of God's name. So I refused. Thursday passed without incident. The preacher faded into oblivion. My acquaintance never spoke to me again.

✧

I, the Teacher, when king over Israel in Jerusalem, applied my mind to seek and to search out by wisdom all that is done under heaven; it is an unhappy business that God has given to human beings to be busy with. I saw all the deeds that are done under the sun; and see, all is vanity and a chasing after wind. What is crooked cannot be made straight, and what is lacking cannot be counted. (1:12-15)

The word *God* finally makes its appearance in the book of Ecclesiastes. The tone is odd. Ecclesiastes speaks of God with ease and familiarity—but exasperation too. He wonders if God has decreed people to idle away their time on earth without much of a clue about their purpose or goals or ways to accomplish them.

The word *God* shows up in different guises throughout the Old Testament. Each Hebrew word registers a different divine attribute or mood. The most important is YHWH, the name God revealed to Moses, a word so immensely powerful and reverential that it is never to be pronounced. Other names appear: *El Elyon* (exalted, transcendent), *El Olam* (the everlasting), *El Shaddai* (God the one of mountains, the omnipotent), and *Adonai* (my Lord, or Lord of all the earth).[2]

The book of Ecclesiastes uses only the name *Elohim*, the most frequent name for God in the Hebrew Bible. The word suggests Creator, Lord of the universe, Judge, God of the vast distances. *Elohim* is so sacred that it must not be erased once it is written or printed in a book. (Six other names for God are treated this way: *El, Ehyeh-Asher-Ehyeh, Adonai, YHWH, Tseva'ot,* and *Shaddai.*) Old and tattered Hebrew texts containing those names of God are not to be destroyed but buried or stored away in a respectful manner when it's time to discard them.

The twenty-first-century list of English words and images of God only grows and mutates. A pluralistic era of big-bang geophysical speculation and Internet spirituality stirs the imagination: Lord, Father, Mother, Eternal Spirit, Earth Maker, First Cause, Companion, Holy One, Divine Absence, Lifegiver, Great Unknown. Behind these words lurk definitions and hunches of the ultimate divine. They seem to multiply daily. Here are a few:

- God is the ultimate source of awe, demanding prayerful silence.

- God glows through Jesus Christ as personal Savior; the divine is accessible as real presence in bread and wine or baptism of the Holy Spirit or ancient painted icon.

- God is totally other, unknowable, hidden.

- God is supreme micromanager; winner of hearts, battles, and football games.

- God is the infuser of everything, the undergirder of all.

- God is mediated through sacred text.

- God is known in fiery, hand-clapping, celebratory worship or not at all.

- God is found in the face of others, in suffering.

- God is found in prayer.

- God is found in speculation, in rational proofs.

- God is met in miracles.

- God is known in the sheer gratitude for daily life, sunrises, mountain ranges, Mozart.

- God is ultimate friend, confidant in the dark, always whispering back.

- God is known in the waiting for God.

What's Ecclesiastes' view? Like a forgotten holy man in a cave, Ecclesiastes is out of step but undeterred. He praises God as Creator and Lawgiver whose providential hand gives us all we see. But God is inscrutable too; Ecclesiastes insists I not forget that. Ecclesiastes charts a different path from prime-time religion. He does not rehearse the traditional biblical stories of God's intimacy with Israel, God's mighty acts on behalf of the chosen people. Those stories are told elsewhere. Instead his role is to probe, testify, contradict, summarize God's relationship to human experience. Ecclesiastes' code of conduct turns away from the overheated holy gossip that carries the day. We'll see if he succeeds.

> I said to myself, "I have acquired great wisdom, surpassing all who were over Jerusalem before me; and my mind has had great experience of wisdom and knowledge." And I applied my mind to know wisdom and to know madness and folly. I perceived that this also is but a chasing after wind.
>
> For in much wisdom is much vexation,
> and those who increase knowledge increase sorrow. (1:16-18)

The word keeps showing up: *wisdom.*

The book of Ecclesiastes is considered wisdom literature, one of a handful of other books from scripture that fall under the category. Proverbs, Song of Solomon, and Job are the others. Wisdom sounds like something lofty to attain, difficult, perhaps out of reach of everyday life unless you sacrifice job and weekends, have a mountaintop experience, and read all the right books.

No. Wisdom in biblical times meant something closer to the ground, according to scholars—practical guidance, peace of mind, mastering one's routine, learning the ways of the world, based on respectful fear of the Creator of all.

The search for wisdom is for anyone. The God of wisdom gave people intellect to remember the big picture, understand the order of things, and find their place in it. Wisdom literature made no special reference to the sweeping drama of salvation history. Instead, wisdom is full of advice on how to get on in this world, avoiding folly and self-defeat. In the wisdom framework, the human search for truth comes from the inside, from experience. We can know the world and live a life that makes sense.

Yet even wisdom has limits. This verse delivers one of those moments—an obnoxious subversion of wisdom, the never-remarked truth that sometimes thoughtful study leads to sorrow at the hard facts of human folly and self-destruction, blindness, tragedy. Greater wisdom comes, sometimes, through the negation of wisdom.

Wrapping up chapter 1, Ecclesiastes refuses to soar upward and declare reconciliation and tidy closure. Instead he offers militancy. I look for a twinkle in his eye, some sign of hope, but I don't see it. He follows his own thinking to wherever it must lead, however desolate or disconsolate. All is vanity, he insists. But this is not the end. It's only the beginning. Chapter 1 isn't the last word.

CHAPTER 2
BLUES MEMOIR

I said to myself, "Come now, I will make a test of pleasure; enjoy yourself." But again, this also was vanity.

—Ecclesiastes 2:1

Over lunch one day, between the salad and the entrée, an influential clergyman told me that God had arranged to delay the sale of his house until the real-estate market improved. Everything worked out in the end because God oversaw the transaction. God made it happen.

He was sincere, expressing gratitude for how well life was chugging along just then. I've heard this story many, many times—homage to the personal ministrations of the Almighty. I do it. I thanked God the other day for our safe return from a Scotland vacation, including the Scottish car rental adventure of nervously driving a total of 777 miles on the left-hand side of the road all week long—somehow without a scratch, thank God.

A question lingers: Where's everybody else in the story whenever we thank God for personally seeing us into safe harbor? What about the miseries of the rest of the world? If I give God credit for hitting the jackpot on the house sale, then how is God relating to the less-fortunate-than-us? The wretched of the earth—the infant casualties of war and disease, the hundreds or thousands who died of starvation that very hour during the buffet special—what about them? Are they the spiritual have-nots with no similar access to God's micromanagerial services? Are they the losers in the spiritual sweepstakes of God's blessing? What about the millions dead from every human ordeal—the 15 million dead in World War I, the more than 25 million dead from the flu epidemic of 1918 (550,000 in the USA), the 55 million dead in World War II, the nearly one million dead in the Rwanda massacres, the 550,000 dead in Angola's civil war, the untold thousands killed in Iraq during the last decade, the 200,000-plus dead after the Asian tidal wave? These voiceless others don't enter into the calculations.

Americans hold a bedrock belief that God loves us with a special intimacy. A professionalized motivational style of speaking dominates the religious mainstream. The style is confident, brisk, invulnerable, bullish, and inattentive to the details of faraway suffering while summoning the Almighty to endorse every need or desire. Only when such instigators themselves crash against inevitable family tragedies or personal failure do they discover the weather of suffering, a theology of the real world, new levels of compassion.

Writing about religion over the years, I've conversed with people of every brand of belief. I've met believers who carry their faith with singular good humor and integrity—mountaintop visionaries, healers, homeless people, ecstatic dancers, denominational staffers, antihunger advocates, laypeople of all sorts—and the occasional authoritarian personality and manipulator. The latter are easy to spot: they must win every argument about God, every war of words. They carry on long filibusters of prophecy and assertion, brooking no compromise or consensus. And if God meets their noisy moment with silence, they are happy to finish the sentence for God.

Their press releases never cite the book of Ecclesiastes—his probings of spirit, desolations, and insights. Ecclesiastes works an alternative road through the heart of faith. In chapter 2, he offers something new, a kind of memoir, the only one in scripture, a pilgrimage of vulnerable self-discovery, an experiment of the senses, a tour on the road of ornate excess in order to test the odds of redemption there. He embarks with questions, not answers.

This is the only place in scripture where a narrator remarks on such an odyssey so openly, without fear of admitting his false starts. He affirms reverence for God even without a clear phone line to the Lord.

Ecclesiastes' detractors say this is his mistake, his weakness: he turns away from the Lord's living presence in a haze of pessimism, like a crusty lone ranger of the spirit. But the neglecters of Ecclesiastes overlook something—his seriousness, his unstoppable respect for God and God's laws. Nowhere in the Bible is such a quest for the wisdom of God laid down with this sort of candor, detail, and contempt for the usual rules of public testimony. Life is not a game of debate points. It will not be varnished by false cheer. God is Ecclesiastes' creator, not his realtor.

I said of laughter, "It is mad," and of pleasure, "What use is it?" I searched with my mind how to cheer my body with wine—my mind still guiding me with wisdom—and how to lay hold on folly, until I might see what was good for mortals to do under heaven during the few days of their life. (2:2-3)

The memoir continues, a remembrance of things past, an ancient exercise in autobiography, recounting a royal catalog of riches and opulence from a never-never land of autocratic excess. No wonder he claims the fearful authority and bottomless coffers of a king. Who else would have access to such abundance? I'd find him hard to believe otherwise, and hard to take.

The tell-all aspect of his narrative resonates with the twenty-first century. We're in an age of memoirs. They're a publishing phenomenon, rivaling novels for readers' attention. Fiction is losing its power to describe scarcely believable reality. The five-million-dollar birthday parties of the rich, the world-threatening diseases, the dating rites of Internet relationships, the medical breakthroughs, the sudden tsunamis, the terrorism of the new century—no novelist could keep up with the astonishments of real life.

Memoirs suit the times for another reason. In an age of pluralism and fragmentation, no one can sum up the world anymore.

The memoir's first-person voice gives the reader a companion in the adventure of discovering this life.

Ecclesiastes offers such a first-person viewpoint, a voyage of self-discovery in defiance of religious tradition. And his story is a blockbuster. He writes like an eyewitness to the cataclysms of Genesis, like a man walking the earth the day after the disaster in Eden, the expulsion from the Garden, the Fall of humanity. He talks as if stunned and shell-shocked by the ordeal of cosmic punishment, the event described early in the book of Genesis that cursed human beings to a life of toil and a destiny of death, and now he surveys the damage, learning to live with the consequences of sin—the spiritual frustration and physical death that define the human condition after Adam and Eve.

Ecclesiastes writes as if the original separation from God is a fresh wound and he's tailoring his words to fit the new reality. If we take the Bible to heart, we shouldn't dread Ecclesiastes. He only articulates what we worshipgoers say we believe: the world fell into sin long ago, and we inherit its ruins. Ecclesiastes takes the Genesis story of creation, the ramifications of the human stain, as seriously as anyone writing in sacred scripture.

Little did he know his memoir would find a spot in the biggest best-seller of all time.

I made great works; I built houses and planted vineyards for myself; I made myself gardens and parks, and planted in them all kinds of fruit trees. I made myself pools from which to water the forest of growing trees. (2:4-6)

So who is Ecclesiastes? The answer is never conclusive. Through the ages, he has been described as an aristocratic country gent, a Bronze Age existentialist, a democratic radical, a careerist philosopher in a Jerusalem academy, a tutor to the children of the rich, a cosmopolitan Jew who followed Greek intellectual trends, a wandering charismatic marketplace rabbi, a tired old bon vivant looking back on a full and turbulent life.

The business of Ecclesiastes' identity is fancy guesswork at best.

Scholars gamely put forth conjectures and hunches. It's a small industry in itself.

If he really was Solomon, why does the book never call him Solomon at all but Ecclesiastes and Qoheleth? The Hebrew name *Qoheleth* remains a mystery. It doesn't appear anywhere else in the Bible. It could be a title for a teacher who gathers an assembly. Or maybe Qoheleth is related to the word for harangue. That would be fitting. Recent theories say the word *Qoheleth* refers not to a person at all but to the book itself, an "assembly" of pages of wisdom.[1]

We don't know who Qoheleth was. Thank goodness. If we knew the details of his life, then Freudians, Marxists, and postmodernists all would have stepped in long ago to dismiss Ecclesiastes' arguments as the sputterings of psychological repression or socioeconomic bias.[2] There's no way to escape it: every theory about Ecclesiastes reflects the preoccupations of current times. A recent argument insists he was not one person but at least three, maybe ten, which would explain the inconsistencies of the text. In an age of staff meetings and team building, perhaps it's comforting to think of the book of Ecclesiastes as a committee project, not the effort of one cantankerous individual single-handedly questioning the system.

So a slight air of embarrassment hovers over any discussion of Ecclesiastes' identity: Here in the globalized age of 100 million Web sites and a trillion search-engined facts at our fingertips, we know practically nothing about the identity of one of the authors in the biggest book in history. Things that have divine imprint elude us.

It's better that way.

> I bought male and female slaves, and had slaves who were born in my house; I also had great possessions of herds and flocks, more than any who had been before me in Jerusalem. I also gathered for myself silver and gold and the treasure of kings and of the provinces; I got singers, both men and women, and delights of the flesh, and many concubines.
>
> So I became great and surpassed all who were before me in Jerusalem; also my wisdom remained with me. Whatever my eyes desired I did not keep from them; I kept my heart from no pleasure,

for my heart found pleasure in all my toil, and this was my reward for all my toil. Then I considered all that my hands had done and the toil I had spent in doing it, and again, all was vanity and a chasing after wind, and there was nothing to be gained under the sun. (2:7-11)

I see Ecclesiastes as an aging man on the steps of the city square, staring off after dismissing his bevy of students, and remembering his earlier life with bewildering pain. Things were good, then they slipped away or mutated into something nightmarish.

To travel with Ecclesiastes' mood and outlook is to grant yourself permission to find the bottom of forbidden fears and linger there—where anxieties rumble under lock and key in the dark, those dreads about sudden death, or divine judgment, regrets of a lifetime, a feeling of creeping chaos. I know of no other sacred document in our culture that invites a reader into the shadows like this to face the darkness for a time.

After 9/11 Ecclesiastes could have been music to regain our strength. Soon economic routine and politics slipped back to normal, except now we made room in the psyche for a new element: a contaminating dread, the silent daily worry of deadly terrorism. The twenty-four-hour news channels kept us permanently on edge, and color-coded terror alerts dictated the national hue of daily outlook like a metaphysical mood ring.

How did the world get into such a fix? We don't talk about it. Our dependence on foreign oil, our support of the repressive governments that supply it—we don't talk about it. Instead, all sides of the debate claim God on their side, a convenient way to justify conquest, mass murder, disdain for the suffering of others.

To read Ecclesiastes is to establish a beachhead on a different shore, a place of self-confrontation under the clarifying blaze of the sun, with nowhere to hide amid the endless sands of time.

So I turned to consider wisdom and madness and folly; for what can the one do who comes after the king? Only what has already been done. Then I saw that wisdom excels folly as light excels darkness.

> The wise have eyes in their head, but fools walk in darkness.
> Yet I perceived that the same fate befalls all of them. (2:12-14)

For a brief moment the reader is tempted to breathe easier. Ecclesiastes seems to be talking normally. He appears to prize wisdom over folly. Perhaps he is at last playing the role of reassuring sage.

But no—the last line is a rumbling cloud of trouble: death happens equally to wise persons and fools.

Death befalls all. Well, we knew that. But the way Ecclesiastes expresses this truth is ominous. He has been declaring "all is vanity," and he means it. His logic leads him to this jarring emotional place, where moral distinctions are mowed down. Death cancels every gain, he complains. Ecclesiastes is winding up to hurl his most shattering fireball into the face of humanity and religion.

> Then I said to myself, "What happens to the fool will happen to
> me also; why then have I been so very wise?" And I said to myself
> that this also is vanity. For there is no enduring remembrance of
> the wise or the fools, seeing that in the days to come all will have
> been long forgotten. (2:15-16)

There, he said it. It's no better to be wise than foolish. Everyone dies just the same—destination oblivion.

Many have tried to make sense of Ecclesiastes' awful moment of bleakness. They hope to soften the blow with rational explanations. Theories abound:

1. He is a disagreeable old man who should not be taken too seriously.

2. He is really a secret idealist, a poet hurt by disappointment. His hotly bitter outburst is a dead giveaway for the buried idealism he still harbors in his heart of hearts.

3. His fatalism symbolizes an intellectual crisis in the Israel of his day. The prophets are dead, and the nation is overwhelmed by defeat and disillusion. A feeble national faith can no longer supply an answer to his

rage and grievance. He has no way out of his misery because no new ideas are available, no salvation.

4. He did not author this negativism at all. His dark words are the quotations of an opponent in a running dialogue with him, not the sentiments of Ecclesiastes himself.

If these theories don't fly, here's another one: Ecclesiastes never existed. The angry and inconsistent remarks in the book were gathered by an anonymous author and placed in one jumble of a scroll, then dedicated to Solomon—an omelet of desolation to keep readers scratching their heads for thousands of years.

These theories all have one thing in common: they're evasive. They avoid the prospect that a real person residing in the Holy Bible, carrying the authoritative glow of the Word of God, dared to vent sizzling emotions at God and us and the laws of mortality. It's a mood of the spiritual life that everybody has known, without having received written permission from the authorities. Until now.

So I hated life, because what is done under the sun was grievous to me; for all is vanity and a chasing after wind. (2:17)

This passage feels like the low point of the whole book, a low point in the Bible itself. There's nowhere to go now but up, and the great challenge, for writer and reader both, is the climb to better light and air—if there's still strength to sweat it out.

It cracks open a dirty little secret about our relationship with the Holy Bible. Despite reverence for scripture, hardly anyone reads all of it. Despite its slot right after Psalms and Proverbs and before Song of Solomon and the Major Prophets, Ecclesiastes never makes the A-list. Rare is the church that reads this slice of the Good Book in public.

This verse is a big reason why. Nobody's happy with it. Some Bible commentaries avert their eyes, skip over it in silence.

It reads like the flash of a suicidal moment. Ecclesiastes could have stopped at the dead-end road where his outburst deposited him and remained there. But rather than collapse, he mastered the moment. It passed—like the wind, like a vain emotion. He decided to hang around and see how it will all come out in the end. He made a bid for permanence. He said yes to life—and to us, his wondering descendants. He wrote the book of Ecclesiastes.

> I hated all my toil in which I had toiled under the sun, seeing that I must leave it to those who come after me—and who knows whether they will be wise or foolish? Yet they will be master of all for which I toiled and used my wisdom under the sun. This also is vanity. (2:18-19)

The word *vanity, hebel* in Hebrew, continues its march across the pages. Other modern translations replace *vanity* with up-to-date words, trying to get closer to the intended meaning. Instead of "This also is vanity," other translations say, "This too is meaningless" (NIV) or "It is all useless" (GNT) or "This too is emptiness" (NEB).

English has a hard time capturing the ever-so-fragile wispiness of *hebel.* As noted already, the word does not mean inflated ego or conceit. In the original Hebrew it suggests vapor, breath, transience, something unreliable, impermanent, vanishing. *Hebel* is apparently a wordplay on Abel, the first person in the Bible to die.

Contemporary biblical word choices for *vanity*—"emptiness," "useless," "meaningless"—already sound a bit musty and dated, smacking of undergraduate despair or moth-eaten modes of 1970s existentialism. They're not quite accurate either. The word *vanity,* on the other hand, somehow keeps its corrosive bloom, a negative grandeur, even four hundred years after the King James Version made it famous. The Bible has the market cornered on the word. It hurtles through the centuries, accumulating mass and velocity. If you feel, as I do, a slight sting of reproach at the word, a withering look, you know it's arrived on target once again.

> So I turned and gave my heart up to despair concerning all the toil of my labors under the sun, because sometimes one who has toiled with wisdom and knowledge and skill must leave all to be

enjoyed by another who did not toil for it. This also is vanity and
a great evil. (2:20-21)

Occasionally I meet a Christian or Jew who has no opinion
about the afterlife. It's always a shock. Such believers are preoccupied by a wholly different spiritual drama—the claims and demands
of this life. In their eyes this life blazes with wonder, meaning, and
need. So they profess no anxiety, no curiosity even, about their own
postmortem destiny. They are serene about the future. They put it
in God's hands—end of story. They contemplate God for the divine
being's own sake. They find something eternal in that.

When I meet such a person, I am chastised. I am suddenly aware
of how easy it is to treat faith like a business transaction, a long-term
profit strategy, a heavenly retirement plan, and lose sight of the stew-
ardship of life on earth, the created world that survives me. It's the
style of everyday religion in an intensely pragmatic society—fearful,
self-involved. I've been that way as long as I can remember. Most sermons, most beliefs, are caught up in the question of where we and
our loved ones will spend eternity. When was the last time a sermon
urged compassion as its own reward?

Furious, Ecclesiastes registers his wounded sense that unfair-
ness triumphs and impermanence goes unredeemed. No doubt he
would turn to heaven for such redemption if he thought he could.
But he does not.

The "heavens" were part of the Israelite imagination from early
times. Heaven is where God lives. Only gradually did the idea evolve
that heaven might also be a destination for human beings. Second
Kings 2:11 states that the prophet Elijah was gathered up to heaven
in a whirlwind. Later, other biblical prophets were granted visions
of heaven and access to its secrets about the righteous and the
wicked.[3] By the time of Ecclesiastes, fuller concepts of heaven were
entering the bloodstream of Israel; the sufferings of Jewish history—all the persecutions and martyrdoms—triggered longings for
divine consummation and ultimate healings in eternity.

Ecclesiastes represents the old tradition—in which death means
dispatch for both the righteous and the wicked to the shadowy

underworld, Sheol, the realm of the dead, a place separated from God. Ecclesiastes, perhaps, was the last Israelite to shout at heaven—to aim his angry sense of injustice at heaven—without expecting heaven to answer.

Today when I meet believers who refuse to devalue the present by measuring it against some doctrinal horizon of the future, I'm amazed. They evangelize by example. They trust God; they are fearless. Ecclesiastes is their patron saint.

What do mortals get from all the toil and strain with which they toil under the sun? For all their days are full of pain, and their work is a vexation; even at night their minds do not rest. This also is vanity. (2:22-23)

"Even at night their minds do not rest." During a recent night of restless vexation, I perused the writings of atheists.

I do this from time to time—read nonbeliever writers like Gore Vidal and William Gass. They are useful. I admire their passion, their self-searching honesty.

They can be harsh. They think it's folly that a loving God would create AIDS or allow us to invent nuclear warheads. They think it's a waste of time to believe at all.

They remind the believing world that there are other conclusions, other nightmares. I read them to know their best arguments. They force me to sharpen thoughts and senses. They write with flair. Would that more believers communicated with such aplomb.

Unbelievers intimidated me as a kid, the rare times I met one. I wondered if they were more courageous than I for proclaiming such unpopular convictions. Today, I confess, I enjoy them for another reason: besides the heroic exertions, there's something a little comical about their spewings. There's something futile and hapless, this lonely rage against God, against the dark, the vastness. No matter how articulate, they end up screaming against an ocean—the ocean of belief and Bible mystery, the faith of a billion hearts at once, the eons of religious poetry and epiphany, the sheer thatness of four thousand years of prayer and wonder etched into the very stones of the earth beneath the sky-filled silence of the

Creator, God's necessary invisibility on the canvas of the world. It's bigger than they are, and they know it.

Many such atheists unfortunately are tempted to regard all religion as "fundamentalism." They have no time for nuance and distinctions. It all stinks. They lazily ignore Ecclesiastes and his thunderous, contemptuous dissent against sentimental piety.

Atheists often end up trafficking in caricature and self-caricature, based on helpless memories of unlucky religious experiences from childhood. But such writers are part of the divine comedy too. They bear the image of God despite themselves.

There is nothing better for mortals than to eat and drink, and find enjoyment in their toil. This also, I saw, is from the hand of God. (2:24)

Do you read this passage with surprise, delight, relief? Or confusion, annoyance, disgust?

The world might be divided into two kinds of people, depending on how they react to this verse from Ecclesiastes. The choice comes down to two basic interpretations of the world, two ways of regarding Ecclesiastes' entire project.

One side will say Ecclesiastes' position is defeatist resignation: it's a paltry, unworthy philosophy of life to say physical pleasure is the best we can do.

The other side will see things more positively. In a sacred canon dominated by ancestral dramas and redemptive visions of the future, here is a rare word for the dignity of the present moment. Seize it; seize the good you find today, known by the senses and underwritten by God; all else is vain speculation.

This is Ecclesiastes' report on the human condition: Our limited mental, emotional, and physical equipment is the gear God gave us for God's own reasons. It's not designed to know the mind of God but to observe the world, learn from experience, live wisely, and praise its Creator.

This is an early turning point in Ecclesiastes' wanderings. It may take time for this passage to sink in. It flies in the face of every humorless stereotype of religion. But it's not so strange as it sounds.

In the Bible, food and drink symbolize celebration and God's blessing on a nation. First Kings 4:20 hails the reign of Solomon as a time when "Judah and Israel were as numerous as the sand by the sea; they ate and drank and were happy." Instead of bearing gloom, Ecclesiastes reminds readers what the Bible actually says about blessing and gratitude. Verse 24 is worth repeating—a modest endorsement of, yes, the life of the senses. If it sounds shocking, it's only because puritanism still has its grip on the American religious imagination even after almost four hundred years. Puritanism preached the total depravity of humanity and equated sin with crime.[4] It rules our doctrinal and political debates to this day. If Ecclesiastes can knock a crack in the thick wall of this unchallenged religious reflex, then I know he and the Bible are doing something right.

> Apart from [God] who can eat or who can have enjoyment? For to the one who pleases him God gives wisdom and knowledge and joy; but to the sinner he gives the work of gathering and heaping, only to give to one who pleases God. This also is vanity and a chasing after wind. (2:25-26)

I ran into a religion professor friend who asked what book I was working on.

"Ecclesiastes," I said, bracing for an eruption.

"Are you kidding?" he replied. "Why would you possibly do that?"

Ecclesiastes makes the professors uneasy. Ecclesiastes doesn't compute. Why must it be in the Bible at all? It's full of trouble. Everything was humming along just fine until Ecclesiastes showed up.

This passage typifies the mess Ecclesiastes creates. It's a wilderness of guesswork. Experts aren't sure how to take it. I ran across three irreconcilable scholarly hunches this afternoon:

1. This passage is about divine predestination—the idea that God has arbitrarily prearranged everyone's fate, for good or ill, without consultation or appeal.

2. It's a defense of goofing off. Those who work and gather and reap end up serving those who don't, so why bother to work too much?

3. The passage was added later, long after Ecclesiastes'
   time, by a pious editor who wanted to boost the number
   of references to God in the book.

What we do know is that ancient Wisdom literature in the Bible
was deeply preoccupied with righteousness, with earthly rewards
and punishments. Traditional wisdom said everything's right with
the world: good people get their reward here, and God grinds the
evildoers into dust. This is often the message of the book of
Proverbs, located directly before the book of Ecclesiastes.

Qoheleth begs to differ. By his time too much had happened.
A long history of Israelite tragedies and backsliding, foreign occupation and the scattering of believers, gave Ecclesiastes doubts that
the divine law of earthly rewards and punishments worked. The
age of the prophets was over. The old religion wore thin under foreign domination, with a widening gap between rich and poor.

Today, despite every secular pretension, people worry about the
justice of rewards and punishments as much as any biblical era. Theological questions are seldom aired in public these days, but they still
haunt us, a debate we mostly keep to ourselves: "Am I worthy?" "Are
coincidences signs of divine intervention?" "Why is God punishing
me?" "Will God forgive me?" "Why am I here?" "Why did my friend
die so young?" My sense of fairness is easily offended. I expect the
order of things to reflect a just world (the year-end bonus for work
well done, credit where credit is due, and prison time for tax evaders,
murderers, public defrauders, and other misery mongers).

But these are strange spiritual times—lots of politicized religion but also a drift from traditional patterns of belief and practice
toward something as yet unnamed. What about heaven and hell,
those destinations of ultimate reward and punishment? There's no
longer consensus about what they mean. They aren't discussed
with the confidence of previous ages. Churches don't agree about
them. Heaven and hell are seldom preached in the fiery terms of
yesteryear, despite the occasional country church marquee that
grimly urges, "Turn or burn."

Rationalists say humankind will one day outgrow a hankering
for the afterlife. They always underestimate the religious reality. A

2004 Gallup poll revealed that 70 percent of Americans believe in hell; 81 percent believe in heaven.[5] Those numbers have risen in the last decade.

The spiritual life can be a lonely thing when organized religions announce conflicting stories, and the broader culture is distracted by fame and fear. The loneliness is not so different from that of a sage named Ecclesiastes writing twenty-three hundred years ago. As chapter 2 ends, an attitude gains steam and clarity: Human life is in flux; the only reliable fact is that of God, the greatest fact of all. God is inscrutable, but God's world grants the rest of us room to roam and discover purpose and delight.

CHAPTER 3
ANTHEM OF THE WORLD

For everything there is a season,
and a time for every matter under heaven:
a time to be born, and a time to die;
a time to plant, and a time to pluck up what is planted;
a time to kill, and a time to heal;
a time to break down, and a time to build up;
a time to weep, and a time to laugh;
a time to mourn, and a time to dance;
a time to throw away stones, and
a time to gather stones together;
a time to embrace, and a time to refrain from embracing;
a time to seek, and a time to lose;
a time to keep, and a time to throw away;
a time to tear, and a time to sew;
a time to keep silence, and a time to speak;
a time to love, and a time to hate;
a time for war, and a time for peace.

—Ecclesiastes 3:1-8

The world wakes each morning to the clash of one thing after another: music, mortar fire, cool breezes, scary headlines. It's hard to carry it all around in one brain. The clang of contradiction wants to drive each of us crazy in our own unique way, "a time to seek, and a time to lose."

Then reality further lowers the boom. My father died. He was eighty-two, worn down by kidney failure, dialysis, and high blood pressure. Death had been closing in for months, years. Still it was all a shock. He had a sharp mind and a big heart. He was the family provider, a petroleum engineer who worked deep in numbers but loved Mozart, Brahms, and his family.

Just before Christmas, he checked in to the hospital with a touch of pneumonia. Within days he became disoriented, then suffered heart failure. By the end of the weekend he faded away. We were with him every day, monitoring the slow, then rapid, decline. I saw him in the hospital bed five minutes after he died—his body's turmoil and fatigue had finally given way to earthly stillness. The grief at his death was a torrent for my mother and all of us. But he had reached past eighty. Would that any of us live that long. I could only be grateful for his gentle and generous ways, his lasting love for my mother and his two boys.

Before the funeral, my uncle, my mother's brother, called from Kansas City.

"I don't know yet if I'll make it there, but you must do this: read Ecclesiastes 3 at the service," he said.

We had read Ecclesiastes at my Uncle Leo's funeral on the western Kansas plains four years before.

"You should do it for Paul too," my uncle said. "And if I don't get there, I'll sit down and read it out loud wherever I am when the service starts."

He was right, of course, to make the recommendation. And he did arrive in time for the service. And we did read this long, famous passage. And it all made sense.

At first Ecclesiastes' words look like the pitiless, gnawing friction of opposites, life's maddening paradoxes. Yet when you read them again and again, they take on the power of ritual, accounting for life's big moments, the pattern knit into the universe itself, the long train of time moving through every living being in every sort of weather, carrying the imprint of the Lord's plan to its destination. The rhythms of God's creation will not be denied.

Hearing these words at the church funeral, amid the churnings of grief, I slumped a little with relief. Somehow someone had dared to write such phrases despite the human urge to gloss over the bad news. Verses 1 through 8 fall like soft rain over the landscape, bathing everyone within earshot. The passage identifies miracles of love and art and also the awful facts of war, evil, and mourning. Ecclesiastes has recovered his vigor again here at chapter 3—enough to compose one of the great poems of the Bible and of literature.

Some commentators see nothing but big-time pessimism in this poem: everything is predetermined by God, and we have no clue as to when or why. They say Ecclesiastes offers no light.

These are prim arguments, abstract, tidy, bloodless. Ecclesiastes' doubters should hear his words at the funeral of a loved one. The verses add up to an anthem of the world. They lend a sense of ceremony to the zigzags of life, the sudden turns, the moody face of inevitability itself. His poem transfigures sorrow into something like acceptance, maybe even healing. It grants permission to admit the obvious—the hard flow of grace and danger on the banks of the river of time. It has the power to sanctify.

Ideologues of war and peace will seize on only one side of Ecclesiastes' poem—the "kill" part or the "heal" part, the "mourn" or the "dance"—not conceding its opposite. Ecclesiastes' poetic roll call of paradox rings truer. We march into firestorms one day, sunshine the next; life is a jostle of stress, release, and wonder.

Dad's death brought sadness, numbness, dread, pride, and thanks—all at once. Hearing Ecclesiastes, I hold it all together and make peace for a while. His poem makes one thing plain: suddenly "time" is no longer something I don't have enough of. In fact it's more than I can handle; it's an overwhelming torrent. Everything flows down its banks, every memory, a merciless flow. In a rounded-out lifetime, we will come to know life's DNA and flight pattern, followed by a messy unceremonious departure, the shocking unadorned fact of death laid out before you in a hospital room, without trumpets or commentary. Yet once death happened, it wasn't death I was left thinking about but something else—holiness. Looking at my dad, five minutes gone, I thought that this dying was holy. His life, and now his death, were holy because they were irreplaceable, given and now taken by God. Every life and every death is that—unrepeatable, unique, holy.

Ready or not, we learn life's inventory of holiness in conditions of heavy weather. This is the storehouse of life, a story God had in store all along.

ॐ

What gain have the workers from their toil? I have seen the business that God has given to everyone to be busy with. (3:9-10)

Is Ecclesiastes un-American? This passage seems like a jab against the American work ethic, against the humming momentum of the economy, our crossroad of striving and creativity.

Americans are optimists. Taming the wilderness and going to the moon required optimism. Every new wave of immigrants reinforced the view that tomorrow, or next week, will be better. A worldwide poll by the Pew Center in 2002 showed Americans to be the most optimistic people on earth. Pollsters asked for reaction to this statement: "Success in life is pretty much determined by forces outside our control." Most countries glumly agreed with that—France, Kenya, Russia, China, Turkey, and others. Americans disagreed by over 60 percent. Most Americans believe their own choices and hard work determine personal success. Our destiny is largely in our own hands. Health and wealth await.

This is individualism's article of faith: the self is heroically equal to the obstacles of the world. The self will not be denied. It never occurs to anyone that limitation might have the last word. New religions have always sprung up on American soil, new can-do doctrines of spiritual abundance. Homegrown theologies offer positive thinking, mind over matter, the inner light, unstoppable daily miracles, the overthrow of Old Europe's jaded weariness. Traditional faiths are updated to fit boundless new expectations—we take what we need from them and fuel the hungry engines of the self. Jesus walks with *me;* he talks with *me.*

Along comes Ecclesiastes. What does he offer? Reminders of limit, death, dust, vanity, simple truths of mortality. But people look to religion for good news, not bad. Why talk of limit? Limit is not part of the American story. The New World's story is about invention and reinvention.

But wait. The American soul has always had a shadow side, a counternarrative that complicates the optimism. If opportunity was born anew here, so was Puritanism, with its fierce view of human sin, the depravity of us all under the implacable judgment of God. Echoes of this old religion never died away. We still carry them around in our genetic history. "Repent now" billboards, the best-sellers about Armageddon and redemption, the all-night tent revivals—these testify to unease about the soul of the nation, its materialism, celebrity worship, and secret addictions.

This head-on contradiction of Puritan pessimism versus Founders' optimism has sparked America's restless creativity ever since. Ecclesiastes' words are never totally alien. An Old Testament river still flows in the veins.

We've been blessed with natural resources and an ethic that maximizes potential. What if resources run out? Domestic oil production is declining. What if the work ethic dissipates? Will the next American epoch be one of difficult limits? Ecclesiastes stands by, his vigilant realism never out of date, ready to accompany readers through the next five minutes or the next five hundred years.

He has made everything suitable for its time; moreover he has put a sense of past and future into their minds, yet they cannot find out what God has done from the beginning to the end. (3:11)

The first time I read verse 11, my knees buckled. I realized no one would ever surpass it as a summary of the human predicament. It describes why I'm never quite at home with myself, why we dream big and press forward but never quite reach the ideal. It's a time capsule of human nature.

Other translations drive home the point of this verse better than the NRSV. An earlier translation, the Revised Standard Version, leaves a vivid impression, despite the old-fashioned male pronouns: "He has made everything beautiful in its time; also he has put eternity into man's mind, yet so that he cannot find out what God has done from the beginning to the end" (Eccles. 3:11, RSV).

"Eternity in the mind." That phrase explains everything, every vision and its distortion—the dreams, delusions, poetry, prayers, suicides, Gregorian chant, religious wars, sainthood, rock concerts, every act of compassion. The taste for transcendence, the seeds of hope, are planted in the human soul. It's where the dream of peace comes from. Genesis says we are made in God's image. This is the location of the image of God upon us, this "eternity in the mind." It's our choice every hour, to honor it or tarnish it.

Eternity flickers on the periphery of vision. There's no way to lay hands on it or keep a steady grip on the wheel for long. People slip and veer off in one direction or the other—moments of transcendental ecstasy or the ash of finitude that follows.

A casino is a great laboratory for chasing the dream of eternity. But it goes astray. The loud, revved-up simulation of everything— the boozy, festive neon; the jackpot hustle; everyone hunkered down dead-serious on a stool at the slots or the blackjack table, trying to stay upwind of a dank odor of disappointment—speaks to an ultimately disappointed religious dream of freedom and release. Debt and resentment get in the way.

Every day I wade into light or darkness, searching for the face of God or mistaking it for a usurper, a pretender, the face in the mirror. It's the daily prospect: a glimpse of eternity, brightly lit or fatally distorted, lies behind every burst of extraordinary art and murderous illusions too. Beethoven had eternity in his heart. His music reminds us we have it too.

In less than forty words, Ecclesiastes outlines the meaning of being human. God makes "everything beautiful in its time," Ecclesiastes now declares. How far we've come from his earlier scream about hating his life, just a few verses ago.

I know that there is nothing better for them [people] than to be happy and enjoy themselves as long as they live; moreover, it is God's gift that all should eat and drink and take pleasure in all their toil. (3:12-13)

Robert Louis Stevenson said, "There is no duty we so much underrate as the duty of being happy." A duty to be happy? It's a funny thing to say. Duty sounds like a chore, something to put off till later, a responsibility out of step with individualism, consumerism, and . . . happiness.

Happiness a duty? As if we could make ourselves happy by sheer automatic will. Isn't happiness more unpredictable than that? It's more likely to arrive without warning—on the shoulders of a deep-blue-sky morning or a pop song or a loved one walking into the room.

This is no great era of happiness. Addiction, divorce, corporate betrayals, and extremism break millions of hearts. Science and prosperity, as it turns out, aren't persuasive deliverers of happiness. The multiplying choices of a consumer society require more and more time to research the right option. The unintended consequence is more anxiety, not more happiness. The quest for spiritual happiness is one of the biggest news stories of our time.

Even if they find it, some people aren't comfortable with happiness. They're sure they don't deserve it. They don't trust it to last. They are the full-time self-employed in the all-consuming business of self-hatred.

Ecclesiastes proclaims something counterintuitive, repeated from chapter 2, and it won't be the last time either. He'll say it seven times in his book: God's purpose for us is to enjoy the good that surrounds us in daily work, in daily pleasures and friendships, in food and drink—a theme Robert Gordis explores in his book *Koheleth: The Man and His World.*[1] These are God's gifts. We should receive them, be their stewards. To be happy is our God-given duty.

It's confusing to hear this statement when religion's traditional message is sacrifice and renunciation. Happiness on earth is considered a dubious goal, something feckless and unreliable. Suffering is the surer path to heavenly happiness. Festivity, emotion, and passion look vaguely suspect in the halls of many a respectable faith.

But Ecclesiastes isn't making things up as he goes along. His notion of the goodness of creation, the duty of happiness, springs from the first verses of the Bible itself, the big drama in the book of Genesis, where God created the world and said it was good. God created the heavens and earth for God's own mysteriously cheerful reasons.

It's the sin of pride to choose misery over happiness. It's our duty to pull up others with good cheer, which has a way of pulling ourselves up too.

⌘

> I know that whatever God does endures forever; nothing can be added to it, nor anything taken from it; God has done this, so that all should stand in awe before him. That which is, already has been; that which is to be, already is; and God seeks out what has gone by. (3:14-15)

At the moment, the air is lousy with "a time for war" sentiment. "A time for peace" is far away. Fear of terrorism, uncertain oil supplies, Iraq's shaky future, the sinkhole of Mideast hostilities—this is our burden, the new emotional interior, the hollowed-out place where we do our walking-around thinking and fretting.

Reading Ecclesiastes, I strike a little truce with myself, a brief rest from the exhausting labor of fear, the dread daily geopolitical chore of absorbing the latest outrageous news, the latest atrocity. This passage shows Ecclesiastes at his most religious and faithful. The disdainers of Ecclesiastes' message, the denouncers of his "pessimism," sound like a conspiracy of ignorance and ill will.

" . . . so that all should stand in awe before him," Ecclesiastes says.

Awe is at center stage. The twenty-first century, this dazzling and dangerous place, isn't comfortable with religious awe. It offers glittery substitutes, objects of awe of our own making—the wizardry of cloning and video games, the shock-and-awe scale of cruise missile devastation seen on the glowing wide-screen TV.

Religious awe implies something else—a time to shut up in the presence of an inconceivable divine power. Time to stop condemning, stop arguing. What follows from awe is silence.

A religious encounter with awe is still the secret goal. People yearn for it whether they know it or not. Instead society gets—or chooses—bottomless fear and its fraternal twin, puffed-up certitude. Some claim to possess the divine blueprint for the whole world, and they make a living urging everybody else to embrace it. The religious think tanks, talk shows, pollsters, and lobbyists add to the throbbing economy of media chat, revving up resentments, distorting facts.

So it's consoling to read about the indestructibility of God's work: "I know that whatever God does endures forever; nothing can be added to it, nor anything taken from it; God has done this, so that all should stand in awe before him," Ecclesiastes says. Human-made toys are designed to wow and intimidate, but they destroy as often as they create. I prefer indestructible divine awe to the human sort.

Moreover I saw under the sun that in the place of justice, wickedness was there, and in the place of righteousness, wickedness was there as well. I said in my heart, God will judge the righteous and the wicked, for he has appointed a time for every matter, and for every work. (3:16-17)

This passage marks a new section, a new direction: Ecclesiastes turns his gaze outward to the political world. He cares after all. He's been keeping up with the news, observing how the world works and who's running it. And he's alarmed. Wickedness resides where justice should. The rich grow richer on the backs of powerless people who have no land or rights or representation. Exploitation of one over another—it's an old story.

It's tempting to dismiss cries for justice as a bumper sticker cliché ("No peace without justice"). Dismissals make life easier. But an inconvenient fact gets in the way: the Bible says believers have responsibilities to the poor. Before Ecclesiastes' time, scripture enshrined the rights of poor people in Deuteronomy and elsewhere. It's the heritage of the Exodus: the powerless Israelites were saved from Egyptian tyranny by God's justice, and now it was their duty to remember the underdog as they built their own society.[2] Sabbatical years (every seventh year) were established to give fallow land to poor people and cancel their debts. Laws were put in place to restrict interest rates on loans to lower-income people.

Within a few generations, by the eighth century BCE, the idealism of the law had fallen into ruin. Prophets noticed. They shouted against social injustice and warned of catastrophe if Israel did not heed God's will and respect the poor. Israel would pay dearly for its lapses. By 587 BCE, the Holy Land was shattered. Israel was invaded; thousands were dragged off in captivity. This conquest was seen as God's judgment. By Ecclesiastes' time, perhaps 250 BCE, Israel had been restored, but foreign occupation continued, and so did a downward spiral of the body politic. Exploitation was a feature of an entrenched aristocracy—slavery, primitive wages, no advocacy at the level of central government, no social security or economic bonuses.

The Bible makes dangerous reading. It sets readers face-to-face with ethical expectations in the real world. The temptation is to spiritualize what gets read in the Bible and swerve around the political ramifications. It would be nice to turn to scripture and shut out the tarnished daily world. So much else in life has become divisive and politicized—media, family relationships, denominational agendas, sermons. It's too much—loud, angry, accusatory, fretful.

But the Bible insists. Ecclesiastes confronts his readers with talk of the "place of justice." He will not have it otherwise, and he will burn it into us until we won't have it otherwise either.

> I said in my heart with regard to human beings that God is testing them to show that they are but animals. For the fate of humans and the fate of animals is the same; as one dies, so dies the other. They all have the same breath, and humans have no advantage over the animals; for all is vanity. All go to one place; all are from the dust, and all turn to dust again. (3:18-20)

Every year in deadest winter, I find myself in a church pew on a special weekday, Ash Wednesday, when we all file up to the altar to get a bit of ash imposed on the forehead by a minister who intones Ecclesiastes' theme: "You are dust, and to dust you shall return." The words roll like thunder through public religion every year, on the first day of Lent, the forty-day Christian season leading up to Easter.

"Remember that you are dust, and to dust you shall return," the minister declares to each of us. The words echo from Genesis 3, which is what Ecclesiastes had in mind here. Dust is our destiny. What can a mortal say to that? There's no time to argue, no argument to be made. Only God is God. Ash Wednesday is an annual corrective, a reality check, a rebuke against comically human arrogance. (Jews, each autumn, have their own version: Rosh Hashanah and Yom Kippur, the Days of Awe.)

In the Episcopal church I attend, the ash ritual is followed by a prayer that embodies Ecclesiastes' spirit while adding the Christian claim of life everlasting, with Christ trumping the dust: "Almighty God, you have created us out of the dust of the earth: Grant that these ashes may be to us a sign of our mortality and penitence, that we may remember that it is only by your gracious gift that we are given everlasting life; through Jesus Christ our Savior. Amen."[3]

Ecclesiastes' words are clear: Dust is the great equalizer. Death explodes the fiction that some people are better than others or deserve to exploit others. All people die, indeed like animals. The shadow of death gives us two unexpected gifts: perspective and compassion. This creates a link between morality and mortality. Death is not just the awful unknown but a teacher, a messenger that all life is holy. No one has a divinely ordained advantage over anyone else— all die equally. No one has the right to superiority. Death discredits pretension and pomposity.

Would Ash Wednesday exist without Ecclesiastes' theme of dust and mortality? The early church, sensing a need for eloquence to meet the first moments of Lent, found in the old scriptures a blazing passage that transfigured the penitential season and the narrative of life itself. It became Ecclesiastes' gift to Christian liturgy.

Who knows whether the human spirit goes upward and the spirit of animals goes downward to the earth? So I saw that there is nothing better than that all should enjoy their work, for that is their lot; who can bring them to see what will be after them? (3:21-22)

Ecclesiastes introduces two little words that never get a hearing in public talk about religion: "Who knows . . . ?"

Organized religions provide answers. Their job is not to leave us with questions. Once again Ecclesiastes moves against the grain. He ends his chapter with a question, a cry of exasperated impatience: Who can possibly chart the trajectory of the human spirit at the moment of death? It's vain and pointless to try; doing so leads only to religious arguments that divide or even kill people. It shores up misplaced aggressive doctrinal "answers" without clear biblical evidence. We are not meant to know everything. Where do birds and deer and all the others go once they die? Mysteries trail into deeper mysteries. I think Ecclesiastes is relieved to know he doesn't need to know.

So he again says his mantra: Enjoy your work. It's what you can do. Ecclesiastes puts his hope in God, not in feverish vanities of knowledge. Hope is not the same as knowledge. Knowledge must constantly be updated, upgraded, canceled out, and revised. Hope lies beyond human fiddling. It is not competitive. It doesn't depend on the latest flashy discovery, which will only be superseded and forgotten when the next one comes. Czech statesman-writer Václav Havel once defined hope as the assurance that life makes sense regardless of how it turns out.

Ecclesiastes' words—"So I saw that there is nothing better than that all should enjoy their work, for that is their lot; who can bring them to see what will be after them?"—add up to a statement of faith. Hope is belief that this world's sufferings and dreams make sense in the largest scheme of things. Hope says all will be revealed one day. It all makes sense in the end.

CHAPTER 4
RICH AND FAMOUS

Again I saw all the oppressions that are practiced under the sun. Look, the tears of the oppressed—with no one to comfort them! On the side of their oppressors there was power—with no one to comfort them. And I thought the dead, who have already died, more fortunate than the living, who are still alive; but better than both is the one who has not yet been, and has not seen the evil deeds that are done under the sun.

—Ecclesiastes 4:1-3

From the opening words of Ecclesiastes, the reader is invited to hang on for a wild ride, an adventure, a struggle, a question that never ends. If you believe scripture carries authority and embodies truth, then what to make of the book of Ecclesiastes?

Ecclesiastes tests everybody's spiritual comfort level. Is the book of Ecclesiastes God-inspired, God-breathed? Did God bless every word? Is it holy? Is it true? Is it the "Word of God" in the same way as other books of the Bible? Can a person embrace the hard-edged spirit of Ecclesiastes and still be a good Jew, a good Christian? Or is Ecclesiastes a bizarre mistake, an aberration, a curmudgeon who slipped past security and wandered into the holy corridors of the canon?

"All things are wearisome . . ." and "For in much wisdom is much vexation . . ." and "So I hated life, because what is done under the sun was grievous to me"—Ecclesiastes is full of passages that embarrass any picture-perfect version of biblical orthodoxy. Yet his book is part of the sacred canon. And now, in chapter 4, Ecclesiastes takes a different line of attack—a heartfelt outburst on behalf of the oppressed. He implies we should do something about oppression.

I read every sentence of Ecclesiastes as if the Bible's stoutest public defenders are right when they say scripture should be taken as truth. There's no use pretending Ecclesiastes and his passionate warnings don't exist. All right then: Who were the oppressed, and who are they to me?

Today the word *oppressed* hardens into a mere slogan of culture war—a faceless, boring abstraction. Conservatives and liberals might argue about how best to help the oppressed, yet the hardscrabble lives in the world's teeming poverty zones seldom merit a headline or a close-up in the land of big-corporation media.

In biblical times the poor were not a distinct social class or political movement but a ragtag collection of people strewn across Israelite society, including slaves and ex-slaves, people just barely getting by one way or another.[1] *The Anchor Bible Dictionary* catalogs six categories of poor person in the Hebrew Bible or Old Testament and counts the number of references for each:

- peasant farmers, mentioned forty-eight times
- beggars, mentioned sixty-one times
- the "lazy poor," cited thirteen times, mostly in the book of Proverbs
- low-income laborers, mentioned twenty-two times
- the politically exploited and oppressed—mentioned most often in the Old Testament, eighty times

At this writing, an estimated 30 million Americans earn less than $8.70 an hour, the official U.S. poverty level for a family of four. These "working poor" are not so faceless after all. We interact with them every day. These aren't the homeless hunkered under the bridges. They're clerks in discount stores, malls, cafés, secondhand shops, and upscale businesses too—wherever people work for low wages and no benefits.

It's a political setup we all participate in, as critics of the system point out. All those bargain-basement prices we expect come at a price—to the employees. "Their low-wage, no-benefits jobs translate into billions of dollars in profits, executive pay, high stock prices and low store prices," declared *The Nation* magazine in 2004. *The Nation* profiled an Alabama woman who works as a nursing assistant at a nursing home for $700 a month. She works the night shift, emptying bedpans, tending the bedridden, mopping floors, and doing other tasks beyond her job description because the place is understaffed. She can't afford a car, so she pays someone else to drive her thirteen miles to work. If that person doesn't show up, she walks. Better to walk than call in sick and probably lose her job, she says. She lives alone with her three children in a shack. There's no phone. The toilet's in the floor. The heater is broken. But she likes her work. She likes to make the residents smile.[2]

Others caught in the poverty grind are practically unemployable: they're damaged victims of self-defeat or prejudice or poor education or abuse. Ecclesiastes' "tears of the oppressed" continue their flow from his day to this.

Mexican theologian Elsa Tamez finds something terribly current about Ecclesiastes. The world's vast sweatshop class of workers in the global economy is ready to hear Ecclesiastes again, she says in *When the Horizons Close: Rereading the Book of Ecclesiastes.*"The Book of Qoheleth or Ecclesiastes has become timely again today, when horizons are closing in and the present becomes a hard master, demanding sacrifices and suppressing dreams."[3]

In his time, Ecclesiastes dispensed advice to a culture not unlike Tamez's Mexico: he spoke to people living in a province in the shadow of empire. He wrote from a small colonized country during the spread (or "globalization") of Hellenistic Greek ideas and commerce and technology, radiating from large foreign cities like Alexandria. Ecclesiastes is a "renegade aristocrat under foreign domination" who has lost hope in the old ethical vision of the Hebrew prophets to resist the dominate powers of his day, says Tamez.[4] Behind his frustration at life resides a half-hidden utopianism, a postponed dream of justice and material goodness. He grieves, unable to connect with any reform movement. All he can offer is his eloquence for enjoying the good of the present moment, and sympathy to the downtrodden who are manipulated by the powerful. What Ecclesiastes lacks at the moment is a hopeful, long-haul plan of resistance, a utopian horizon of God's redemptive reign in human affairs, Tamez argues.[5]

What about "utopian horizons" today? Do they exist? The twentieth century will be remembered for the rise and fall of massive, disastrous human secular utopias and ideologies—notably, fascism and socialism. Only one ideology is left standing in the twenty-first century: American-style capitalism—and its angry opposite, anti-Americanism. No other economic vision can rally people's passions.

Does any economic system speak compassionately to the poor? Nothing about my daily routine makes me a worthy advocate, I have to admit. But to take the Bible seriously is to remember what the unpredictable Ecclesiastes is doing here: giving a voice to people who don't have the means to enjoy their work, their moment, under the sun. Suffering people in Ecclesiastes' time lacked the same thing they lack today: belief in a future tense of hope and someone to mobilize their numbers into a political power to get the attention of a distracted world.

Then I saw that all toil and all skill in work come from one person's envy of another. This also is vanity and a chasing after wind. (4:4)

The seven deadly sins—can you name them?

Church fathers compiled the traditional list (technically it's not found in the Bible) some fifteen hundred years ago, and it hasn't changed since. The seven prove their remarkable durability with every passing day under the sun. All seven manage to explain everything behind this morning's headlines.

1. *Greed:* The pay gap between big-company CEOs and average workers now is around 300:1. In 1982 it was 42:1.

2. *Gluttony:* Nearly 65 percent of Americans are overweight or obese.

3. *Lust:* Without it, the colossus of advertising would collapse this afternoon.

4. *Sloth:* It's easier to follow the boxers-or-briefs details of favorite movie stars than to fight for clean air, pure water, and a hundred other matters of public urgency.

5. *Anger:* Terrorism is another name for the hopeless rage that defines the times.

6. *Pride:* We go to war now on the belief that cheap foreign oil is an American birthright.

7. *Envy:* Ecclesiastes chooses this one as the engine that revs up the day's hustle, bustle, getting, and spending.

The seven deadly sins are difficult to separate. Each feeds on the other. Envy triggers anger, which leads to greed or sloth. Gluttony, lust, and pride seem to come as a package. Ecclesiastes wants to give envy pride of place. I won't argue it. It's usually the one I'm least willing to admit to. Etching it into the Holy Bible itself, he ensures envy will always be in the lineup of seven deadly culprits of human misery.

Fools fold their hands and consume their own flesh.
Better is a handful with quiet
than two handfuls with toil,
and a chasing after wind. (4:5-6)

Fools—it's an old-fashioned word, a little musty sounding. It hardly seems equal to twenty-first-century needs and outrages. We seek insults with more bite: moron, idiot, or the latest multicolored palate of obscenities that lodge deep in pop culture's vocabulary. Today they're a psychological expectation, as if the obscene scale of misdeeds to describe—financial rip-offs, mass destruction—demands no less.

Fool has been demoted to dupe, buffoon, tool. Fool for love. Fool's gold. Nobody's fool. April Fool's Day gives the word its only dignified public forum, preserving an outmoded, almost Shakespearean meaning as trickster, clown, office fall guy.

In the Bible, though, *fool* has a serious history, and Ecclesiastes draws on all the shame and ridicule the word carried in antiquity. A fool is no mere idiot but something much worse, someone who denies God, scoffs at wisdom, laughs at eternity. Foolishness is a theological stance, a show of contempt for the laws of God. Ecclesiastes' nice phrase "a handful with quiet," an attitude of respect and reverence, is always lost on fools.

To condemn someone as a fool in biblical times was thus a serious matter, an abusive, damaging term. Psalm 14:1 declares, "Fools say in their hearts, 'There is no God.'" Jesus warned of dire consequences to anyone calling anyone else something as awful as a fool: "If you say, 'You fool,' you will be liable to the hell of fire" (Matt. 5:22).

Ecclesiastes takes his chances. He aims and fires.

Again, I saw vanity under the sun: the case of solitary individuals, without sons or brothers; yet there is no end to all their toil, and their eyes are never satisfied with riches. "For whom am I toiling," they ask, "and depriving myself of pleasure?" This also is vanity and an unhappy business. (4:7-8)

It becomes clearer now that chapter 4 is about work—and how we distort it. Scholar Ellen Davis notes four ways work gets perverted: oppression (verses 1-3), envy and idleness (verses 4-6), and overwork (verses 7-8).[6] They all conspire against the enjoyment of a day's work and exertion, which is God's gift and ours to savor if we could see past the boredom and competitiveness.

A preacher could devote a year of sermons just to the question of what scripture teaches about work, labor, and money. The most famous statements come in Genesis: labor was natural even in paradise, where Adam tilled and kept the garden of Eden. Work became burdensome and hard only after the Fall, when God punished Adam and Eve for violating the divine instructions and straying from the ground rules of their original innocence.

Other biblical statements clarify proper attitudes about work. The fourth commandment puts a limit on it: keep the sabbath, it says. Keep the day holy by interrupting work's egotistical endeavors. Rest and recharge creativity. In the Sermon on the Mount, Jesus urged against worrisome strivings: pursue first the kingdom of God; don't store up treasures on earth.

Ecclesiastes adds his voice to this slate of warnings. Oppressive overstimulation distracts from the present moment, the only thing real, the only moment that puts a person closest to God.

It will take a revolution of the mind, an overthrow of the heart, to hear these words again as simple truth.

> Two are better than one, because they have a good reward for their toil. For if they fall, one will lift up the other; but woe to one who is alone and falls and does not have another to help. Again, if two lie together, they keep warm; but how can one keep warm alone? And though one might prevail against another, two will withstand one. A threefold cord is not quickly broken. (4:9-11)

Ecclesiastes' tone shifts; suddenly he speaks in proverbs. His rhythms are simple and direct. Folk proverbs are commonsense sayings, the homespun wisdom of the ages. The book of Proverbs is partly a collection of such sayings.

This chapter began with a series of questions: Is the book of Ecclesiastes true? Is it inspired? Is the Bible inspired? What does that mean? This passage from Ecclesiastes looks sensible and self-evident, whether you read it as a defense of marriage or as simple advice about being neighborly.

But what about the tougher passages, the difficult and stupendous themes found throughout scripture—the miracles, the thunderous words of God, the troubling outbursts of Ecclesiastes? *The New Interpreter's Study Bible* identifies no fewer than seven definitions of biblical inspiration, seven different ways that people choose to read the Bible every day. Here's a summary of the seven positions, paraphrasing Robert Gnuse's article "Inspiration of Scripture":[7]

    1. The very words of the Bible are inspired by God. The text is without error in all matters of faith, morals,

history, and science. An inerrant Bible is necessary for the sake of certainty in theology, ethics, and belief.

2. The Bible's original manuscripts were error-free. Modern scholars may find errors or inconsistencies in the translations and texts that have come down to us.

3. The Bible is infallible in matters of faith and morals but not in matters of history and science. God communicated religious truth to finite human beings in specific ancient cultural settings. Scripture may contain inaccuracies but is free of deception.

4. Only the ideas, not the actual words, of scripture are inspired. The words are the fallible product of people in their historical era. Despite its mixture with potential human error, the Word of God still speaks authoritatively because of its origin in God.

5. Only the original experiences of the prophets, apostles, and historical figures were inspired, not necessarily the literature written in their name, which came long after the original personalities spoke.

6. The Bible is not equated with the Word of God, though it may contain the Word of God. Rather, the Word of God is found in the living voice of a congregation or faith movement, not in a book. The inspiration of God occurs in an encounter between God and believer. Scripture can be said to be inspired when it speaks to an individual.

7. Divine inspiration is found in the entire effort of producing, assembling, and reading the Bible—all the personalities, scribes, editors, and faith communities who contributed to the emergence of scripture, and those who engage scripture today by reading and living by it.

Seven roads to relating to the Bible adventure—must they be mutually exclusive? In my experience they intersect and overlap.

Nearly everybody—left-wing, right-wing, devout, moderate, skeptic, even atheist—will take one part of scripture or another very literally, ignoring others. The rules of the road allow for left turns, right turns, U-turns, detours, and alternative routes to the destination. The question of biblical inspiration and interpretation is a big one, *the* big one. It divides believers, splits congregations, fuels culture wars. It burns inside the heart of faith, worthy of a lifetime's struggle and enlightenment, undertaken with seriousness and alertness. But there's no need to dread the ride. Look out the window and enjoy the view.

> Better is a poor but wise youth than an old but foolish king, who will no longer take advice. One can indeed come out of prison to reign, even though born poor in the kingdom. I saw all the living who, moving about under the sun, follow that youth who replaced the king; there was no end to all those people whom he led. Yet those who come later will not rejoice in him. Surely this also is vanity and a chasing after wind. (4:13-16)

I admire biblical scholars, rely on their labors, salute their care and tenacity, and eavesdrop on their work. They feed the never-ending drama of sacred commentary, now more than two thousand years old. Every day they grapple with the freeze-dried intrigues and puzzles of silent ancient texts, sifting through their shredded, ribbony remains. They contend valiantly with difficult passages the rest of us shrug at or walk away from. They must attend to minutiae and hairsplitting. This makes academic scholarship a subculture of exquisite caution and sometimes its opposite, one-upmanship.

But we are free to brood and dwell on scripture ourselves. An old monastic tradition of Bible reading, called *lectio divina,* offers the invitation. In Latin, *lectio divina* means divine reading, sacred reading, meditative free-form reading. It's like an eighth way of interpreting scripture, a strategy to add to the seven classic definitions listed in the previous section. Probably everyone practices it at one time or another, calling it *lectio divina* or not—the habit of dwelling on scripture, praying with it, bringing imagination to it, submitting to the Holy Spirit or the presence of God, and letting one's thoughts leap to new connections or insights, all triggered by a phrase or passage. (In her book *Amazing Grace,* Kathleen Norris calls it "a type of free-form, serious play."[8]) This is part of the Bible's power of inspiration, a mysterious pact between reader and text, an ever-renewing relationship across the untold centuries. It's what drives my experiment of reading Ecclesiastes.

So what to make of this opaque passage? What I take from it is an image, the image of the endless instability of public power, the cycle of political commitment, disappointment, distraction, and renewal. Ecclesiastes observes that the restless populace embraces one secular savior after another, a pattern of rise and fall and rise again, with no accumulation of wisdom.

We have our own version of this—the spectacle of the celebrity culture, the glamorous roster of the famous who flood our minds and magazine covers with supercharged urgency, then vanish, to be replaced next week by the next slate of eager contestants for our attention. It takes up more and more time. The well-oiled media give us hourly updates on the shenanigans of fresh-faced personalities and fake-blonde starlets. With our help, they transact a lucrative cultural drama: they get the notoriety or money they seek, and in turn we are dazzled, charmed, or appalled. It's called fame. They produce it; we consume it.

Ecclesiastes' words, "All is vanity" and "There's nothing new under the sun," ring truest and most painfully dead-on when I confront the entertaining and overheated celebrity news in the morning newspaper, on TV and the Internet—who's hooking up with whom, who's suing whom, who's signing the latest $100 million multiyear deal to look pretty in the commercials. This high-priced gossip has taken over airtime that used to go to detailed debates over politics, citizenship, and literature, touchstones that now may be passing. But when I read the Bible, I'm shaken from my corporate media stupor, and I feel like a grown-up again. Scripture beckons to the larger story that's never absent from the background, the story of human destiny and decision.

So let the motions of *lectio divina,* the act of meditating on a strange passage from scripture, take you where it will. The Bible accompanies the willing reader down an unmarked path. Take imagination with you. Ecclesiastes does his part. He arranges a face-to-face encounter with the Bible's power over anyone willing to sit down, face the page, and see what happens next.

CHAPTER 5
"LET YOUR WORDS BE FEW"

Guard your steps when you go to the house of God; to draw near
to listen is better than the sacrifice offered by fools; for they do
not know how to keep from doing evil.

—Ecclesiastes 5:1

What if someone started a "church" of Ecclesiastes? It's not so far-
fetched. The times look ripe. Materialism and science have turned
out to be disappointments. Yearnings for simplicity run deep. So
does a grinding anxiety about the world situation, about the envi-
ronment and the well-being of our own families. Today's religious
climate is friendly to experimentation, extreme worship, alternative services, ancient-modern liturgies—ways of getting closer to
God, closer to the mystery, closer to the bone, away from the
energy-sapping demands of the day's endless routines.

Could Ecclesiastes' defiance serve as a light to the world? What
would the church of Ecclesiastes, the temple of Qoheleth, look like?

How about this:

Worship would follow some basic themes: reverence for God,
gratitude for creation, pleas for forgiveness of vanities and injustices
enacted during the week. Testimonies would be heard. So would
summaries of the history of Israel and the prophets, the shapers of
Ecclesiastes' religious identity. Sermons (kept short) would exalt

75

simplicity, humility, companionship, trust. They would deconstruct fame, workaholism, stinginess, political oppression, compulsive talking. A banner would be unfurled, proclaiming a creed:

- Remember there's a time to live, a time to die.
- All is vanity, but enjoy your work, your days and nights.
- Follow the Ten Commandments.
- We don't know the divine mind, so let's not act as if we do.
- Love God; fear God.

Afterward, a big sumptuous dinner.

Who would come? Seekers, religious refugees, puritans, leftists, traditionalists, malcontents, poets, stoics, musicians, people who meditate, people who grieve.

Half the people I know say they already feel like honorary members of such a congregation. These people stumble upon Ecclesiastes by accident and make him their own. They never studied the book of Ecclesiastes in church. Instead they found it while flipping through the Gideon Bible in the hotel room one night. Or they heard about it in a coffeehouse or at the funeral home. Ecclesiastes is the great word-of-mouth voice in the Word of God.

A coworker breaks out into smiles when conversation turns to Ecclesiastes. She says the great poem that opens chapter 3 saved her life more than once: his words gave her biblical permission to feel the sadness, and also the hope of ultimate answers, when two of her sisters died young in recent years.

"After my second sister died, I was in a bad depression," she recalls. "I was in a place where there's no reason to live anymore. But God showed me that for everything in life there's a reason and a season. I read those words in Ecclesiastes. You've got to be able to accept what's said there, and only then can hope happen. I believe in a sovereign God; those words are in Ecclesiastes for a reason."

Certain issues would have to be worked out before getting this newfangled religion of Ecclesiastes off the ground. The liturgical possibilities look thin. Would there be special holidays? missionary efforts? The cornerstone of Ecclesiastes' teaching is humility—how do you institutionalize that? One of the puzzles of Ecclesiastes is that he turns away from the usual consolations of religion—he ignores the afterlife; he doesn't position earth as a supercharged battleground between salvation and damnation. His energies go elsewhere, to the business of living with integrity under God. There is good to pursue and dignity in work and enjoyment too, ordained by God. Put that on the church marquee.

The New Oxford Annotated Bible (NRSV) says of Ecclesiastes: "Within the biblical canon his book fulfills a necessary role, warning against human hubris and preserving divine mystery."[1] It's odd that these two bone-hard basic conditions of the spiritual life—human humility and holy mystery—would find a mere toehold in the attention span of organized faith. The popularity contests and media coverage gravitate to the opposite theme—religious celebrity, head counts, and sound-bite controversy.

Ecclesiastes offers a dissent. He'll always appeal to individuals who bring bruised questions from the drama of life and want to talk of faith and daily experience with both eyes open. His rigor will never win him a slot on page 1 as the next up-and-coming faith. But the truth is, his "church" already exists as an underground movement. It always will.

Never be rash with your mouth, nor let your heart be quick to utter a word before God, for God is in heaven, and you upon earth; therefore let your words be few. (5:2)

We are moving into the very soul of Ecclesiastes' book, its heart and credo. "God is in heaven, and you upon earth; therefore let your words be few." A thousand books of philosophy slide away. We are put here on earth in search of information. Death is the only long-term, bankable fact. But we keep foraging for deeper truths, testifying, watching, waiting, fighting a lonely feeling, rallying, praying, looking for a sign, gazing up at the sensational sky. It's an awesome business. "Therefore let your words be few."

But Ecclesiastes' advice is hard to take. Everything about the culture, of course, depends on explanation, debate, persuasion, controversy. Language is God's gift. It's the human mark of distinction.

These days, though, something strange is happening. We're testing the human limits of this communications talent: cell phones, chat rooms, and 24/7 news updates keep the talk going into infinity. It's changing society's attitude toward silence—dividing the world into two kinds of people, those who fear silence and those who crave it. Transmission towers are the new towers of Babel.

Ecclesiastes is wary of words. He doesn't trust them. Maybe they've let him down in life. The enemy, in his eyes, is babble. It's a verb and a noun, a word shipped to us directly from the story of Genesis 11, where smart, ambitious ancient people built a tower of brick in the land of Shinar, hoping to reach the heavens and make a name for themselves. God noticed and was not pleased. The Almighty tore down their Tower of Babel and scattered them. Before Babel, people spoke one language. Now, in the ruins, all was babble and confusion as people spoke in many different tongues. Humans had overreached, dreamed too wildly, tried to touch heaven from earth. Verbosity and confusion followed. Ecclesiastes recalls that primordial setback.

I grew up among neighbors whose "words were few"—World War II veterans who lived up and down the street. They never talked about the war. They kept a stone-faced refusal. My dad, who served stateside as a structural engineer at the B-24 factory in Tulsa, never talked about it either. As a ten-year-old, I didn't understand. We had won that war—why not boast about it? Born a decade after Hiroshima and the Holocaust, I regarded the war as the story that haunted everything. There were lots of newsreels on TV—Hitler barking his speeches in Nazi khaki, footage of blitzkrieg, refugees, Germany's defeat in flames. Der Führer's nonstop scowling charisma more than matched any speaker I had ever seen. I associated overbearing personalities with collective brainwashing, the conquest of Poland, mass murder. Hitler gave public speaking itself a bad name.

Much later, when I got to know a few veterans better, I came to realize the nature of their silence. Some were psychologically unable to talk of their experiences, which included killing people and seeing friends on the front line blown to bits. Or they kept silence out of respect for the dead, out of sheer protest that words are inadequate. Or to shame the spirit of the insane Hitler, who desecrated all phrases of honor, sacrifice, patriotism, and sanctity with his incessant, hateful, bloated speechmaking.

God is in heaven, and we are on earth—a place where people dream of peace, and war slices open rivers of blood, and hearts break. Therefore let our words be few. Some people know that better than others.

> For dreams come with many cares, and a fool's voice with many words. When you make a vow to God, do not delay fulfilling it; for he has no pleasure in fools. Fulfill what you vow. It is better that you should not vow than that you should vow and not fulfill it. Do not let your mouth lead you into sin, and do not say before the messenger that it was a mistake; why should God be angry at your words, and destroy the work of your hands? (5:3-6)

Not long ago I was watching one of those cable TV political point/counterpoint shouting matches. The subject was the presidential election—which candidate is the more patriotic, the more likable, the more Christian, the more American? The split screen was occupied by a camera-ready liberal and a conservative counterpart. Both, on cue, got loud and rude. The interruptions were nonstop. Neither was able to finish a sentence. Their snarling five-minute performance aimed to entertain, shock, and tease my boiling resentments to the surface. And it worked. I was irritated the rest of the night. "Do not let your mouth lead you into sin." The debaters' lazy misinformation, the cartoonish posturing, the toxic personal attacks—there was nothing real about it, except that it served to deepen real divisions and confusion among the actual electorate. I take it as a matter of course that the two debaters were all smiles after the cameras shut off, high-fiving backstage, happy to take viewers to record levels of obnoxiousness, before walking off together, sharing the same limo, the same CPA, and bamboozling the same public.

I wondered what their debate would be like if they had staged it not in a New York studio but in a Nebraska wheat field, with no cell phone coverage, campaign footage, or Internet rumors, only the

wind in their eyes and a storm boiling on the western horizon—
God's creation raw and rising at them.

Fools talk too much, and God takes note, Ecclesiastes suggests.
Tell the truth or shut up.

❧

With many dreams come vanities and a multitude of words; but
fear God. (5:7)

One of the most powerful phrases in the whole Bible shows up
tersely here at the end of the sentence: Fear God. It appears four
times in the book of Ecclesiastes like an urgent bulletin.

Bad associations cling to the words *Fear God*. The phrase conjures
up stubborn religious stereotypes, too many angry TV sermons, too
many humorless church marquees on narrow country roads. "Fear
God" goes against the expectation of religious life today, a God-is-
love theology, with access to God's will and timetable. "Fear God" is
not visitor-friendly. It sounds threatening, indiscreet, like a case of
bad manners. In a competitive religious landscape, fear of God isn't
an easy marketing strategy.

But the phrase is unavoidable. It's common sense. Fear God: the
Bible is dominated by it. It's found in both Old and New Testaments.
It serves as a measure of the distance between Creator and creature,
between God and me. Paradoxically, it tightens the human connection to God, lets us know where we stand. The English word *fear*
doesn't really cover it accurately. The Hebrew phrase for "fear of the
Lord" carried a strong mix of awe, holiness, and gratitude, not just
fear. Awe is the brain-hammering experience of the holy, in all its
sudden, blinding surge. Despite the connotations, there's something
liberating about "Fear God." This fear is our friend. It simplifies life,
removes clutter. As the book of Proverbs says, "The fear of the LORD
is the beginning of wisdom" (9:10). So much flows from that belief:
the Ten Commandments, reverence, alertness, caring about neighbor. These are practical things. There's no need to live in the dark—
or in mere fear—after all. Fear, the awesome kind, is the only
sensible attitude to carry around on earth.

If you see in a province the oppression of the poor and the viola-
tion of justice and right, do not be amazed at the matter; for the
high official is watched by a higher, and there are yet higher ones
over them. But all things considered, this is an advantage for a
land: a king for a plowed field. (5:8-9)

I was guest-speaking on the Psalms for a Sunday school class,
talking about the social responsibilities laid out so simply in Psalm
146. It says God wants food for the hungry, help for the orphan and
the widow. God watches over the stranger and loves the righteous.

A man who had been frowning all morning said, "I don't know
what you're trying to say, but the Bible supports capitalism and
free enterprise, and I won't have the government telling me what
to do." His bluntness was impressive. So was the anger he had
brought into the room—a disproportionate disgust at an abstraction called government.

Many, maybe most, Americans have a genetic hatred for Big
Government, a suspicion that flavors every debate regarding education, housing, public prayer, and the plight of poor people.
Antigovernment anger is stoked and fed every day by radio hosts
and op-ed personalities. Conservatives say no to handouts: Let the
down-and-out make their own way up the ladder of success, just
like we did. Liberals say Big Government has a role in easing the
suffering of vulnerable people because no one else will do it.

Scholars aren't sure how to sort out this passage or explain what
Ecclesiastes is up to. He worries (again) about indignities against the
poor. Then he makes a dour comment about the world's entrenched
bureaucracies, a rare biblical remark on the workings of administra-
tive hierarchies. What's his point? Can no one aid the oppressed, and
is government hopeless to try?

I look longingly to verse 9 for a way out, a clue to the meaning,
but come up blank. "But all things considered, this is an advantage
for a land: a king for a plowed field," the NRSV says.

Other translations are only marginally better:

"The increase from the land is taken by all; the king himself
profits from the fields" (NIV).

"But in all, a king is an advantage to a land with cultivated fields" (RSV).

"Yet an advantage for a country in every respect is a king for the arable land" (v. 8, NAB).

"Moreover, the profit of the earth is for all: the king himself is served by the field" (KJV).

I like the King James Version here. It suggests the solution to political wrongs is a stronger relationship to the land. The land is what we all have in common. It's what we all depend on. We hardly give it a thought, since few of us have any relationship to the land or the competence to make it bloom or know any farmers who do. Big-time agribusiness puts farming in fewer and fewer hands. A "theology of the land"—there's no urgency to the idea. The land is mainly what we pave in order to drive as fast as possible to get to somewhere else.

When we run out of oil—in, say, one hundred years or so, triggering war and hardship—the land will matter again. Unless we figure out a new auto-related energy replacement, we won't be so mobile. Local cultivation, local respect for land, will become a matter of survival. Local planning and governance will matter. Community feeling will matter. Perhaps rich and poor will more or less share the same patch of ground and will get to know each other again. Ecclesiastes' words might carry a more powerful charge. His words will be waiting. The problems of the oppressed will be everybody's business again.

The lover of money will not be satisfied with money; nor the lover of wealth, with gain. This also is vanity. When goods increase, those who eat them increase; and what gain has their owner but to see them with his eyes? Sweet is the sleep of laborers, whether they eat little or much; but the surfeit of the rich will not let them sleep. (5:10-12)

A survey stated that most people think their problems would be solved if only they had $10,000 more. That's the figure people settled on. No doubt about it: if I were handed $10,000 of happiness, life would turn rosy. For about ten minutes. That's how long it would take for me to spend it all—for a new roof, a Greek isle cruise, a handful of charities, and the retirement kitty. Then it would be gone. And I'd return to daydreaming about the next $10,000.

Ecclesiastes speaks in truisms here. Everybody knows there's never money enough. Everybody knows the feeling you get at the mall—a giddiness and a sadness. The gorgeous array of things to buy is a glittering miracle of the modern world. So many possibilities, and I cannot have them all, and yet I never quite give up on the possibility, and I know this wasteful struggle between needs and wants will never end on earth.

In her book *The Writing Life,* Annie Dillard declares: "The life of sensation is the life of greed; it requires more and more. The life of the spirit requires less and less; time is ample and its passage sweet."[2] I immediately copied it down, one of those quotes that explains the world. Maybe it shows a way out, the way to step out of the roaring river of getting and spending. Serenity awaits, a place where lightness of spirit prevails.

I think of pivotal moments when Jesus depended on less and less—fewer belongings, fewer rules, fewer words. His burden is light, he said. At times he saw no need to speak at all. In John 8 he was confronted by people who wanted to trick him into a wrong doctrinal answer by demanding that he condemn an adulterous woman to death. He refused to join their debate, instead writing on the ground until the accusers were too ashamed to continue. Later, at his own trial, Jesus gave no answer when Pontius Pilate asked him the famous question, "What is truth?" Jesus refused to take up power or argument or analysis. He embodied the truth Pilate had inquired about. Pilate was too distracted to notice.

Ecclesiastes homes in on maladies that plague the world twenty-three hundred years later—material dissatisfactions, my own restless hypocrisy. I get and spend with the best of them, like a zealous game-show contestant. Greed is a powerful, DNA-level impulse. It motivates achievement; it stands as a law of survival in the economic jungle. It rises with the sun.

But I know something else looms out there, something stronger to those who discover it: the life of the Spirit frees people from the compulsion of grasping and accumulating, and makes it possible to ride the slow flow of time and finally see the waiting world.

Ecclesiastes is a market correction.

> There is a grievous ill that I have seen under the sun: riches were kept by their owners to their hurt, and those riches were lost in a bad venture; though they are parents of children, they have nothing in their hands. As they came from their mother's womb, so they shall go again, naked as they came; they shall take nothing for their toil, which they may carry away with their hands. This also is a grievous ill: just as they came, so shall they go; and what gain do they have from toiling for the wind? Besides, all their days they eat in darkness, in much vexation and sickness and resentment. (5:13-17)

This passage quivers with "much vexation." Riches are hoarded, then carelessly lost. It's a sorry situation. Ecclesiastes evidently alludes to a personal ordeal of some sort—family trouble, perhaps bad financial advice along the way. The final sentence is scariest—the fear of being left with nothing in the dark, nothing but bitterness and loneliness. It haunts him.

Some scholars believe Ecclesiastes had read the book of Job. The passage contains echoes of a Job-like crisis of being stripped of one's belongings. Job's reaction was different. Even after disaster befell him and he got word that all his children had died, Job fell to the ground and declared, "Naked I came from my mother's womb, and naked shall I return there; the LORD gave, and the LORD has taken away; blessed be the name of the LORD" (Job 1:21). His travails deepen through forty-two chapters, until he is visited by, overwhelmed by, the divine presence, and Job repents "in dust and ashes." Ecclesiastes works without benefit of a shattering divine appearance that would set everything aright. What Ecclesiastes does give us, throughout most of this chapter, is a seminar on the hazards of chasing and keeping the big money. Scholar Ellen Davis says Ecclesiastes "shows more awareness of the dangers of amassing wealth than any other Old Testament writer."[3] Only one other biblical personality spoke as plainly and passionately on that subject: Jesus of Nazareth.

This is what I have seen to be good: it is fitting to eat and drink
and find enjoyment in all the toil with which one toils under the
sun the few days of the life God gives us; for this is our lot. Like-
wise all to whom God gives wealth and possessions and whom he
enables to enjoy them, and to accept their lot and find enjoyment
in their toil—this is the gift of God. For they will scarcely brood
over the days of their lives, because God keeps them occupied
with the joy of their hearts. (5:18-20)

Some people are lucky in love. Others aren't. Some are tal-
ented, energetic, long-lived, hopeful, the picture of health. Others
are disfigured by birth defects or suffer mental illness. Thousands
die by earthquake, tidal wave, starvation, car accident, and terrorism, while others waltz safely through nine decades and die quietly
in their sleep. How can we understand the way blessings are dis-
persed, the way the divine moves across our lives, and who gets
what and why and how long, the way heaven and earth relate in
every one of the six billion different life stories?

Questions, questions. Ecclesiastes answers. Enjoy the sunshine;
enjoy work and wealth—these are among the gifts of God to us,
pure and simple, given at God's pleasure. Joy and enjoyment—
bestowed by God for God's own mysterious reasons.

Ecclesiastes is in a quarrel with traditional Israelite wisdom.
That tradition laid down a simple formula about divine rewards and
punishments: we get what we deserve. It's summed up in the book
of Proverbs, which comes just before Ecclesiastes: "The reward for
humility and fear of the LORD is riches and honor and life. Thorns
and snares are in the way of the perverse; the cautious will keep far
from them" (Prov. 22:4-5).

Ecclesiastes rejects the simple equation of good reward for
good behavior. He was writing in a later time, probably as an older
man, whereas Proverbs were written and compiled as advice to the
young. Ecclesiastes arrives at a different conclusion: the seemingly
random distribution of joy and pain is God's prerogative, not ours.
Belief in a sovereign God means we're in no position to question
the will of God. Otherwise we fling ourselves into fruitless deserts

of theological speculation about the motions of providence, and come up with answers that are bound to be wrong and overreaching.

What are these divine gifts? Some people have the gift of enjoying their work without caring how much they make. Or they have a nearly boundless capacity for forgiveness and cheer no matter what their circumstance. Some receive the gift of wealth, others the enjoyment of wealth. This implies some people can't appreciate what they have. In that case wealth isn't God's gift at all but a source of misery, social ill, and destruction.

Joy and enjoyment—these gifts keep surfacing in Ecclesiastes. A gift comes for free, unexpected, no strings attached. But someone must be ready to receive it. The recipient has a choice. Some accept the gift; others refuse. It seems to depend on an infinitely complex mix of factors—background, timing, sense of humor, and sheer energy for overcoming personal hardships.

This is the duty to be happy, once again, the decision to accept the good thing within reach. God's stamp of eternity in the mind of human beings, the image of God, makes choice possible, for good or ill. The number of joyful people—by Ecclesiastes' count, a rather small club—is always fluid, expandable. The gifts are there at the doorstep, ready to be gathered, piling up in greater abundance than we might reckon.

CHAPTER 6
INTERLUDE: HIDE-AND-SEEK

There is an evil that I have seen under the sun, and it lies heavy upon humankind: those to whom God gives wealth, possessions, and honor, so that they lack nothing of all that they desire, yet God does not enable them to enjoy these things, but a stranger enjoys them. This is vanity; it is a grievous ill. A man may beget a hundred children, and live many years; but however many are the days of his years, if he does not enjoy life's good things, or has no burial, I say that a stillborn child is better off than he. For it comes into vanity and goes into darkness, and in darkness its name is covered; moreover it has not seen the sun or known anything; yet it finds rest rather than he. Even though he should live a thousand years twice over, yet enjoy no good—do not all go to one place?

All human toil is for the mouth, yet the appetite is not satisfied. For what advantage have the wise over fools? And what do the poor have who know how to conduct themselves before the living? Better is the sight of the eyes than the wandering of desire; this also is vanity and a chasing after wind.

Whatever has come to be has already been named, and it is known what human beings are, and that they are not able to dispute with those who are stronger. The more words, the more vanity, so how is one the better? For who knows what is good for mortals while they live the few days of their vain life, which they pass like a shadow? For who can tell them what will be after them under the sun?

—Ecclesiastes 6:1-12

Where was God on 9/11? I recently heard a clergyman give a resounding answer: God stayed extremely busy that terrible morning. God was doing everything God could to keep people off those planes (the proof: less than half the seats were filled that day). Without God's intervention, many more would have died.

Could be. I don't know. But it's hard to stop at "I don't know." We must have answers.

Still, I'd rather have no answer than the clergyman's answer. His explanation makes me uneasy for two reasons:

1. It implies that the people who died horribly that day were oblivious to divine warnings, perhaps arrogantly indifferent, while many others heeded the signs and stayed home. Perhaps God chose some to live, some to suffer and die. Either way, the spiritual have-nots went to their doom; the spiritual winners survived.

2. It implies God tried hard but could only do so much. That's a rather limited God.

It doesn't take long to get into trouble whenever conversation turns to God's presence in the human world. The risk is to dishonor God by misrepresenting God, explaining too much, becoming God's spokesperson whether God authorizes it or not.

Ecclesiastes will have none of it. He suspends the rules, rejects the compulsion to explain God's action. What matters is reverence for God. All else is useless speculation. All else, indeed, is vanity. Ecclesiastes goes against a profound instinct of the religious life today—the temptation to treat the Almighty as a micromanaging short-order cook who serves our most trivial whims. When bad things happen, people think God is punishing them.

Ecclesiastes shows another route through the daily spiritual life—awe of God, gratitude for the natural world, not preoccupation with a score sheet that charts God's precise doings and undoings. This won't be enough for some readers. But I am forced to ponder a fact: Ecclesiastes is right there in the Bible. That fact confronts us with the possibility that he may be right.

Ecclesiastes' chapter 6 is short, repetitive, and a little strange. It frets about inheritance—who gets what, and why. The chapter restates a previous message about the sorry limitations of human beings and the importance of enjoying what there is. Undergirding all of it is God, the eternal force who hands us blessings, who watches, who expects an ethical standard to be met.

Who is this God? People carry a billion images and stories of God, but all labor together against one overwhelming limitation. God maintains a fixed, particular relation to time and events—God the Father, the Almighty, remains hidden.

There's an old rabbinic saying: "If God lived on earth, people would throw stones at his windows." This sounds insulting, fatalistic—and true. The whole world cries out God's name, seeks God in every spiritual discipline and physical travail—or unknowingly aches for God in every addiction and all other self-destructive substitutes for divinity. Many an atheist and a believer share one deep assumption: this life would be better if God showed the divine presence right this minute and became visible among us. Then we'd know. No more guesswork, no more blind faith. God could decree clear laws of justice and peace in broad daylight and end human history's central debate. God would finally be geographically accessible, not hidden.

Is this what we really want?

God is hidden—why? Let's linger at the word *hidden*. I can hear the protests against the word itself: The word is too negative. . . . The word suggests God toys with us, plays games with us, and God does not do that. Only an unworthy, unreliable deity would deliberately stay hidden. . . . Anyway, God is not hidden at all. God is in my heart. . . . God is in the natural world. . . . God speaks to me. . . . God blesses the policies of my political party and defeats my enemies. . . . Through the eyes of faith, we see God, so stop this nonsense about hiddenness.

But, metaphors aside, God *is* hidden. No one has seen God. The Lord dwells in heaven, Ecclesiastes says, not on earth. God's voice is not audible, at least not detectable by any normal means. There's no agreement about the real personality of God, the ways of God. We all negotiate this condition of divine hiddenness for ourselves. We pray, read, discern, and act on inspiration to build a case for belief, decision, meaning, mission—or unbelief.

Is this a problem? Of course it's a problem—for lots of people.

I remember, from the time I was five, the sermons by our pastor, who gently decreed the love of God—God's care for us, God's vigilance, God's actions on our behalf in the practical world of rush-hour traffic, baseball box scores, business deals, and family time. I simply took the minister at his word. I believed he told us the truth when he spoke this way Sunday after Sunday, sounding as if God were an invisible personality in our ranks, speaking regularly to us.

Yet our prayers told a different story. Often they were heartfelt requests for God's arrival and attention, desperate pleas to remove suffering and uncertainty—all based on the anxiety that God needed to be summoned, because God was not here after all, not exactly. Our doctrinal belief said, "God is with us"; our behavior said, "We wait for God to arrive; we pray that God will come."

By the time I was a teenager, my confusion was in full flower. I had run up against the limits of metaphor. The presence of God— was that a metaphor or a reality? Was God available or not? No one discussed it. My perplexity and fascination persisted. I see now that I got into journalism in order to keep asking the question, "Where is God, and what does it all mean?" Journalism offered a way to stay in touch with the great search, a chance to see how others navigated through the human condition—the long slate of consolations offered by religion, yet the continued hiddenness of God. After twenty years of asking questions, of writing between two and three hundred stories a year on the subjects of faith, ministry, ethics, doubt, conversion, redemption, heaven, and hell, my amazement at their inexhaustible variations never waned. But I slowly became firm about one thing: the hiddenness of God is a blessing, not a problem in search of a solution.

Thank God for the hiddenness of God. What other arrangement could there be? If God were not hidden, would God be visible? Is visible the same as present? If God were visible on earth, how so? Constantly? Once a year? And where? In the sky of every hemisphere? In Jerusalem? Inside a specific room in a special building in Jerusalem's Old City? Imagine the lines of people who'd queue up to wait to see God, standing in line for years. Imagine all the contradictory requests God would hear.

If God were physically present, imagine a new and overwhelming human burden—the immediate responsibility to do God's will, right now. The Mideast would be forced to find a solution to peace, right this minute—so would every sort of dispute between nations, between individuals. No more delays, no more bitter self-pitying excuses. The Ten Commandments, God's rules, demand it, and God would be here physically to oversee it. What would happen to human freedom if God were looking over every shoulder?

Other questions pile up, brutally: Wouldn't people eventually tire of this miracle of divine presence? We are faulty witnesses. We get bored easily. People being people, would we even be able to agree that this is really God in the first place? Would God be indisputable? Would Jerry Falwell and the ACLU agree? Would the president of the USA and the leaders of North Korea and Iran agree?

Or would we find a way to dispute not only God's presence but God's answers? Would we pester God to give the answer to the great secret, the great question, "What does the future hold—for me, my family, for all of us?" The secret of the "end things" is the one thing we want and can't have, the thing that fills our nights with wonder and fear and insomnia and explains why people try to shore up riches or take drugs—to fill the time, fill the hole, until there's an answer, which only comes at death, or after. Suppose God, living on earth, gave us the answer now—and we didn't like it? Why should God subject the divine holiness to such a fickle crowd? We'd probably throw rocks at God's windows.

Divine hiddenness is hardly a subversive thought. Hiddenness is laced through the Bible itself as a challenge to human expectation, not as an agnostic complaint. The many references to hiddenness in the Hebrew text reflect a worldview: "The mind of Israel was characterized by a profound sense of the hiddenness of things, in marked contrast to Greek thought with its sanguine belief in the capacity of reason to probe the inmost secrets of reality."[1]

The biblical theme of God's hiddenness returns time and again:

- Psalm 13:1: "How long, O LORD? Will you forget me forever? How long will you hide your face from me?"

- Deuteronomy 31:17: "My anger will be kindled against them in that day. I will forsake them and hide my face from them; they will become easy prey, and many terrible troubles will come upon them."

- Isaiah 45:15: "Truly, you are a God who hides himself, O God of Israel, the Savior."

- Romans 11:33: "O the depth of the riches and wisdom and knowledge of God! How unsearchable are [God's] judgments and how inscrutable his ways!"

Divine revelation itself is defined by hiddenness.[2] Revelation comes out from a hidden place, from divine shadows. It's a bolt from the blue, unpredictable, shocking. But even in revelation, God's reasons remain hidden: God does not explain. "For who has known the mind of the Lord? Or who has been his counselor?" (Rom. 11:34).

A reader might object: Jesus was the exception. The Word-made-flesh walked the earth for all to see, and he knew intimately the will of God. Leaving aside the question of how to refer to Jesus' divine status—God the Son, Son of God, the Christ—it is worth noting that he himself said: "I thank you, Father, Lord of heaven and earth, because you have hidden these things from the wise and the intelligent and have revealed them to infants; yes, Father, for such was your gracious will" (Matt. 11:25-26).

For all his restless outbursts, Ecclesiastes remains at peace with a deeply biblical notion: divine hiddenness is God's wisdom for us. Ecclesiastes was, after all, Jewish, not Greek. His style of faith and approach to belief are Jewish, not Greek. Ecclesiastes might gasp and sigh, empty-handed of high-spirited descriptions of God. But he refuses to journey through the wilderness of abstract conjecture about the philosophical attributes and properties of God and prove or disprove God's existence. History, daily life—not philosophical proof—is the place for revelation, the evidence of the divine will, the laboratory of choice and action. The biblical history of Israel became the story by which we understand God's intentions and self-revelation. God the Creator and Sustainer becomes known in the narrative of the Exodus and the covenant. Later the prophets—then, decisively, Jesus of Nazareth—push the story forward, refining God's expectations, God's holiness, righteousness, justice, love, and wrath.[3]

Writing from his own turbulent moment in the life of Israel, Ecclesiastes does not refer to sacred history of Israel or amplify it. He does not borrow its imagery of speaking of God in the usual scriptural way. He looks at what remains, the rhythms of life and the natural world. Because in one spectacular sense God, or God's activity, is not hidden: God's handiwork is visible in sunlight and darkness. That is, the creation. The earth exists; the Bible exists. So does the face of humanity, made in the image of God. Free will exists, the daily choice for good or evil.

Despite his silence about ancient Israel's sacred history, Ecclesiastes remains loyal to Jewish tradition; he refuses to fill the void with hypotheses about the methods of God or the details about future judgment or other "secret" knowledge that leads to sectarian conflict and cult worship. He invites people into the wisdom of restraint.

Ecclesiastes is one of the great witnesses to hiddenness. He does not confuse the hiddenness of God with the nonexistence of God. Ecclesiastes might complain that God is hidden, but he never implies God is absent.

CHAPTER 7
MOURNING GLORY

A good name is better than precious ointment,
and the day of death, than the day of birth.
It is better to go to the house of mourning
than to go to the house of feasting;
for this is the end of everyone,
and the living will lay it to heart.
Sorrow is better than laughter,
for by sadness of countenance,
the heart is made glad.
—Ecclesiastes 7:1-3

Earlier I said I've never heard a sermon about Ecclesiastes. If I had lived in Asia Minor around 380 CE, I would have gotten my fill. An industrious Christian theologian, Gregory of Nyssa (c. 335–c. 394), who was later canonized as a saint, delivered a series of homilies on Ecclesiastes that has come down to us.

The homilies are a remarkable set. Gregory happily tackled Ecclesiastes. He accepted as a matter of course that everything in the Bible was useful to the church. In the New Testament, 2 Timothy 3:16 says, "All scripture is inspired by God and is useful for teaching, for reproof, for correction, and for training in righteousness." The writer was referring to the Old Testament, the Hebrew Scriptures, since the New Testament canon had not yet been gathered into a firm unit. Jesus himself declared, "You search the scriptures because you think that in them you have eternal life; and it is they that testify on my behalf" (John 5:39).

To Gregory, these words were marching orders to dive into scripture for edification, instruction, and blessing—and no skipping over the hard parts. So he gives us a high-spirited reading of Ecclesiastes—no glum sighs over Ecclesiastes' alleged fatalism but a head-on commentary on the first three chapters. Gregory is sure the Christian life can gain from unlocking Ecclesiastes' nettlesome phrases. It won't always be easy, he admits.

"Before us for exposition lies Ecclesiastes, which requires labour in spiritual interpretation quite as great as the benefit to be obtained," he begins.[1]

But we have help. Gregory believed everything in scripture is there for a reason, including the very order of the books in the Bible. The book of Proverbs comes before Ecclesiastes. That's no coincidence. Why? Gregory says the twists, turns, and riddles of Proverbs prepare the mind for the more arduous insights of Qoheleth.

Gregory assumes the author of the book of Ecclesiastes was Solomon, the son of David. With gusto he also refers to Ecclesiastes as Assembler, Ecclesiast, Gatherer, Convener, even Churchman, though Ecclesiastes was a Jew who lived at least three centuries before the existence of any church. Gregory doesn't stop there. By his reckoning, Jesus himself, coming from the house of David, was also a son of David—and therefore was in some spiritual sense the author of Ecclesiastes. In Gregory's theology a kind of mystical mingling takes place, a converging of Christ's identity with all the authors of sacred scripture. If Jesus the Christ was the Word in the beginning and for all eternity, as the Gospel of John says, and if the Bible is the Word of God, then ultimately Jesus is the author of scripture. This reasoning gives Gregory yet more zest and confidence to plunge ahead.

Gregory, famous for his rhetorical skill and defense of the faith in an era of great doctrinal showdowns, was schooled in the philosophy of classical virtue and ethics. He found Ecclesiastes compatible with his own view of the world: he saw Ecclesiastes' text as a book about virtue, how to recognize it, and how to attain it. Doing right, pursuing good—this was the way to pursue knowledge of God—the only way, because there can be no direct vision of God on earth. The purpose of Ecclesiastes was to "raise the mind above sensation,"[2] Gregory wrote, and merge onto the highway of virtuous living.

Gregory was an old ascetic himself, accustomed to a life of monastic austerity, with a minimum of material wants and choices. He had a built-in suspicion of the fickleness of sensual pleasure. It will never satisfy. It will only damage judgment and rational thinking. Better to submit the flesh to the intellect and minimize the constant war between flesh and spirit at stake in the human heart. What about Ecclesiastes' urgings to enjoy food and drink? Unflappably, Gregory turned these into symbols of virtue too. Prudence, he said, is the wise person's food; wisdom is the bread, justice the sauce, self-control the drink.[3]

It's safe to say people don't customarily read scripture this way anymore. Compared to Gregory's imaginative methods of interpretation, we all are literalists today: people take scripture to mean what it says and say what it means, or they take it as poetry, or they don't take it at all. But chances are, modern readers and Gregory would agree on the importance of wisdom to Ecclesiastes, as laid out in chapter 7. Wisdom is the habit of keeping an eye on the big picture: life is temporary; death awaits. Staying mindful of death isn't morbid. It concentrates the mind. It reminds me that time is running and there's work to do. Gregory of Nyssa felt certain that God gives everyone three slices of practical wisdom—the free will to pursue God through virtue, a sense of modesty to keep a healthy perspective, and a sense of shame to control reckless behavior. There's nothing elaborate about these three insights, but they all lighten the spirit. Never would an early Christian theologian and an Old Testament sage agree more.

The heart of the wise is in the house of mourning;
but the heart of fools is in the house of mirth.
It is better to hear the rebuke of the wise

than to hear the song of fools.
For like the crackling of thorns under a pot,
so is the laughter of fools;
this also is vanity.
Surely oppression makes the wise foolish,
and a bribe corrupts the heart. (7:4-7)

My father's death swept up all the family in a sudden, private hurricane of grief. The hour demanded merciless practicality too—planning a funeral, finding key documents, keeping our heads on right. Off in the background, day after day looked weirdly normal—the balmy weather, the bowl games on TV, the unstoppable crush of news in the morning paper. It was impossible to square the familiar rhythms of life with the new information, Dad's terminal absence. The sturdy traditions of bereavement—the guest visitations, the public prayers and eulogies, the graveside liturgies—did their work. They provided Dad's people a place for farewell and an ancient vocabulary of prayer. We were carried along by the great circle of compassion of loved ones.

Only when the funeral day passed did a new flock of real and reeling feelings arrive. After all the food had been put away and the last friends left the house, we had to deal with new beginnings in darkness. We entered the house of mourning.

Ecclesiastes speaks approvingly of the house of mourning. The concept was familiar in the Old Testament. At news of a death, people tore their garments, cut off their hair, threw dust on their heads, and sat on the ground for days.

This isn't exactly the style of the twenty-first century. We baby boomers, for instance, have enjoyed historic levels of distraction from certain truths. Our toys, TV trivia knowledge, record collections, and Beatle memories hardly prepared us for the serious adult business ahead, the demise of those nearest us. The cues from public life weren't terribly helpful either. American society put death in a dark corner, unheard, far from the main arenas of consumer cheer. For millions, the impersonal funeral parlor replaced home and church as the place of choice for a sanitized secular death ritual. An honorable social practice slid away—the traffic ritual of stopping alongside the road to let a funeral procession and hearse drive past. Many lost the habit of writing sympathy notes, letters that exhibited actual personal feeling. It was easy to lose the roadmap to the house of mourning.

So it finds you. The house of mourning is where you sit and wait without glancing at your watch, because the hours no longer matter. You plan nothing, you take control of nothing—not time, not your schedule. Your head swims. Grief, relief, exhaustion all keep returning, doubling back all at once. After a while, you think you're over it. No. The rambunctious emotions fly hidden in the clouds, then dive-bomb from a dozen directions.

Then one morning your eyes clear a bit and you take your vital signs: you're still alive. Alien new thoughts arrive: what I should have said to Dad over the years, how I should have conducted myself better. You become capable of herculean feats of time travel and lawyer-like efficiency: I cast my mind thirty years into the future and see images of my own declining physical state, and how friends and family will adjust to their own long slide. Is everything in order—retirement plans, legal wills? I'm in my forties, sounding like a decrepit ancient burdened by deathbed scenarios: Can the end be dignified? Who will come to the funeral? Who are my friends? What would I do for them? Have I shared enough love? Heaven and hell are two stark, unilluminated planets to confront and make peace with once and for all. Why did God lay it all out like this?

Such is the house of mourning. Soon arrives another unexpected parcel of feeling—strength. New clarity. Purpose. Impatience with frivolity, the calculated titillations of media, the bombastic bad movies. You look around. The truth becomes plain about everybody's big talk and swagger. It's a bluff to hide resentments from seventh grade, fear of the abyss and their own mortality. They're in the dark like everybody else. Without knowing it, they deserve pity. I feel the shortness of time, and it's even a blessing. Only the good stuff matters now—good work, good books, good reasons, good listening, good times with friends and family.

You don't move permanently into the house of mourning. You rent space there. It contains one room, cavelike, unplugged, and that's where work gets done. There I sit on the ground and count the ways. The house of mourning is a school for adulthood, the place to plot the next steps ahead, with the wind of the ancestors pushing from behind. Moving on will mean moving out of the house of mourning but always carrying something of it with me. Dad is gone; we must follow, forward.

⤜⤛

> Better is the end of a thing than its beginning;
> the patient in spirit are better than the proud in spirit.
> Do not be quick to anger,
> for anger lodges in the bosom of fools.
> Do not say, "Why were the former days better than these?"
> For it is not from wisdom that you ask this.
> Wisdom is as good as an inheritance,
> an advantage to those who see the sun.
> For the protection of wisdom is like the protection of money,
> and the advantage of knowledge is that
> wisdom gives life to the one who possesses it. (7:8-12)

All is vanity? Ecclesiastes, despite himself, proves here that all is not vanity: wisdom is not vanity. Wisdom is the protest against vanity. Ecclesiastes offers plainspoken wisdom here without subverting it or questioning it. Each line comes through clear and clean to challenge two ringleading emotions of human folly: impatience and nostalgia.

Lately I'm surprised to feel nostalgia—for the 1970s, the last innocent moment before people became "crazy busy," slammed, covered up. After the '70s, workplace pressures and gadgetry—cell phones, fax machines, overnight delivery, and cable TV—quickened the national pace. So did the deregulation of finance and media. Technology made it possible to chart the minute-to-minute destinies of every stock portfolio. Suddenly people were hurrying with sleep-deprived fear of getting left behind in the big money chase. We started wearing clothes with the designer label showing, a new sign of worry about status. Restaurant going became an event of flamboyant entrées and tall desserts; there wasn't time to fix a meal at home. Civic club membership declined; RSVPs became relics of the past. Twenty-first-century computers, Internet, e-mail, and personal Web sites intensified the furious national style. "Let's do lunch!" I said to someone yesterday, scurrying off, barely waiting for an answer.

So I'm nostalgic. No doubt the '70s were silly and unambitious at the time. But now they look like a decade of decency and sunlight, even despite Watergate. Less noise, fewer culture wars, less foreign oil dependence, no e-spam, no Hummers, no Lewinsky. Food portions were modestly human size. So were CEO salaries.

Nostalgia is bewitching, dreamlike, and appealing. The '70s give me pleasant thoughts. But it's no good. Nostalgia doesn't work. It's bankrupt and tiresome. The stereotype of Ecclesiastes as a defeated old man goes down in flames with this passage. He urges serenity, openness, an embrace of the ticking clock, a rejection of nostalgia, as scholar Ellen Davis suggests.[4] Nostalgia is a snare. It robs the present of its bloom, the next five minutes of its holy potential. Nostalgia dulls the brain to the urgencies of what needs tending in our time, whether family relations or public policy. Ignore these matters, and thirty years from now the burning mess around us will leave us pining nostalgically even for these perilous days.

Consider the work of God;
who can make straight what [God] has made crooked?
In the day of prosperity be joyful, and in the day of adversity
consider; God has made the one as well as the other,
so that mortals may not find out anything that will
come after them. (7:13-14)

Every day I meet people—churchgoers too—who think the devil, not God, rules the contemporary world. They flatter Satan, giving him credit as the secret superintendent of earth. Many believers view the world as a shadowland of supernatural battle, a fight between satanic powers and the Lord. But some people score Satan with the upper hand. Such is the power of personal despair and political discontent. And it's spiritual defeat worse than anything Ecclesiastes ever said.

Ecclesiastes reminds his readers what it means to say God is God. The Almighty is behind everything, the good days and bad. We're not meant to know the unfolding plan. Our job is to do right, fear God, and run with the gift of the present. The sovereignty of God demands belief in a God who is larger than any human hopelessness or "day of adversity." But when things go awry, the human response is to shift into damage control—explain God's reasons, override the master plan, give the impression of mastery of the situation.

Some people equate this mastery of the moment with religion itself. What's the point of religion if an organized faith doesn't provide the answers to every perplexity and give us the last word in any argument? This is the spiritual ecology now, this need for the last word. It's as if few read the biblical prophets or the Bible's wisdom literature anymore, but everyone—politicians, TV hosts, warlords — competes to speak for God.

But if God makes the good days and the bad, then we're disqualified as the official explainers. Jesus threw everybody off balance when he said, "You have heard that it was said, 'You shall love your neighbor and hate your enemy.' But I say to you, Love your enemies and pray for those who persecute you, so that you may be children of your Father in heaven; for he makes his sun rise on the evil and on the good, and sends rain on the righteous and on the unrighteous" (Matt. 5:43-45).

Ecclesiastes protests against the urge to build towering babels of speculation. It's one of his obsessive themes: We don't get the last word. God does.

In my vain life I have seen everything; there are righteous people who perish in their righteousness, and there are wicked people who prolong their life in their evil-doing. Do not be too righteous, and do not act too wise; why should you destroy yourself? Do not be too wicked, and do not be a fool; why should you die before your time? It is good that you should take hold of the one, without letting go of the other; for the one who fears God shall succeed with both.

Wisdom gives strength to the wise more than ten rulers that are in a city.

Surely there is no one on earth so righteous as to do good without ever sinning.

Do not give heed to everything that people say, or you may hear your servant cursing you; your heart knows that many times you have yourself cursed others. (7:15-22)

The book of Proverbs announces the following:

- "What the wicked dread will come upon them, but the desire of the righteous will be granted" (10:24).

- "The hope of the righteous ends in gladness, but the expectation of the wicked comes to nothing" (10:28).

The wicked get what's coming to them? Ecclesiastes has his doubts. He wrote perhaps two hundred years after the compilation of the Proverbs. Much had changed in Israelite society. The old faith was being diluted by a new culture, a new political master: the Greeks based in Alexandria, some three hundred miles away from Jerusalem. Modern experience resisted the old sanctified assumptions. Nonbelievers flourished; the righteous languished.

So Ecclesiastes feuds with Proverbs, scoffing at traditional wisdom's easy confidence in the hope of rewards for the wise and punishment for the unjust. Gregory of Nyssa noticed this. That's why Proverbs comes before Ecclesiastes in the Bible, according to his view. Its simpler instruction warms us up for the testier observations of Ecclesiastes.

Scholar Norbert Lohfink, in his book *Qoheleth: A Continental Commentary*, offers vivid conjectures about Ecclesiastes' situation and attitude.[5] In Ecclesiastes' time, about 250 BCE, the streets of Jerusalem swarmed with competing ideas—Hebrew versus Greek, countryside versus city, stoic versus cynic versus Jewish. Social life was changing fast. The familiar economic pattern of small towns and small farms—the world of the book of Proverbs—was yielding to urban migration and a widening gap between rich and poor. Alexander the Great had conquered that part of the world several decades before; taxation to a foreign power was a hard fiscal reality. Schools jostled for intellectual dominance and influence. Greek schools for young people competed with Hebrew schools. Ecclesiastes, perhaps a charismatic wandering lecturer, had his own set of students meeting on the steps in a corner of the busy marketplace.

There was great pressure to adopt all things Greek. But Ecclesiastes did not cross over, Lohfink notes.[6] Despite his skeptical misgivings about traditional Jewish wisdom, Ecclesiastes committed a fateful act of loyalty to the old ways. He could have written his book in the language of the hip and influential insurgency—Greek. Instead he wrote in the tongue of the ancestors, the language of God spoken to the patriarchs, the chiseled music of the Ten Commandments, the Law, and the Prophets. He wrote in Hebrew.

His is a lover's quarrel with the Bible, and it's why the Bible never let him go.

> All this I have tested by wisdom; I said, "I will be wise," but it was far from me. That which is, is far off, and deep, very deep; who can find it out? (7:23-24)

"That which is, is far off, and deep, very deep; who can find it out?" This is a haunting sentence, a shadow moment that invades the mind on lonely stretches of road and in hospital corridors and at midnight after the storm. It's the kind of darkened honest thought I keep to myself. It shall pass—brightly lit answers will come again—but it always circles around and returns. It is otherwise known as the human condition. The Bible is big enough to include and inhabit such a passage—gracious enough to hand it along and let me make it my own, this mystery of whatever ultimately frightens or intrigues or entreats the heart. "That which is, is far off, and deep. . . ." What is it? The truth? The future? Our very souls? God? It is there and deeply rooted. I'm not going to fear it any more.

> I turned my mind to know and to search out and to seek wisdom and the sum of things, and to know that wickedness is folly and that foolishness is madness. I found more bitter than death the woman who is a trap, whose heart is snares and nets, whose hands are fetters; one who pleases God escapes her, but the sin-

ner is taken by her. See, this is what I found, says the Teacher, adding one thing to another to find the sum, which my mind has sought repeatedly, but I have not found. One man among a thousand I found, but a woman among all these I have not found. See, this alone I found, that God made human beings straightforward, but they have devised many schemes. (7:25-29)

Time and again, Ecclesiastes overturns religious expectations and human assumptions. "The earth remains forever," he says in chapter 1, verse 4, dismissing the apocalyptic mind-set in ancient Israel that yearned for God to destroy the planet and for a new start. "That which is, is far off . . . ; who can find it out?," he says in chapter 7, verse 24, rebuking the professional analysts of everything.

Here, though, he lapses into an age-old stereotype of his time and ours too, portraying "the woman who is a trap" or complaining he cannot find one good woman. Where did this come from? Suddenly we seem to be in the middle of a gender war. Who is he complaining about—one woman in particular or all women?

Some scholars try to rescue Ecclesiastes here: the woman preoccupying him is not a flesh-and-blood lady but a prototype, the mysterious feminine image that haunts the Bible's wisdom literature. Proverbs declares that wisdom has accompanied God from the beginning. This spirit of wisdom, or divine attribute, is embodied in female form—Dame Wisdom. In Proverbs 8:22 a female voice declares, "The LORD created me at the beginning of his work, the first of his acts of long ago." But she has a negative counterpart who shows up elsewhere in Proverbs, traditionally called Dame Folly— and this is the woman Ecclesiastes means. Proverbs 2:16 says, "You will be saved from the loose woman, from the adulteress with her smooth words," a metaphor for whatever distracts a person from pursuing wisdom. So Ecclesiastes' many earlier warnings against folly get rolled up into one great female personification. It is destined to be misunderstood.

If this is unconvincing, there's another argument: Ecclesiastes is speaking at his most personal level here. He is not deriding women but testifying from personal disappointment, bitter rejection, failure to find a soul mate, a life companion. Scholar Ellen

Davis (in her book *Proverbs, Ecclesiastes, and the Song of Songs*) makes this point.[7] It suddenly gives Ecclesiastes a human face. He does not condemn other men who find happiness with a woman. Later, in chapter 9, he urges, "Enjoy life with the wife whom you love" (v. 9). But he did not find married bliss himself. It is hard to know what to make of Ecclesiastes' arithmetic here, but Davis concludes from it that Ecclesiastes was no more successful with male friendships than with female. Loneliness throws a shadow across his life.

This experience might account for the last phrase in this long passage that ends chapter 7. People are capable of "many schemes," tarnishing what God set down straightforwardly. Ecclesiastes has seen it with his own eyes. He makes a heartfelt plea to humanity: stop the madness; walk away from the foolishness; make a change. Is nothing new under the sun? He writes as if a new start is possible, even if not for him.

CHAPTER 8

WISE GUY

Who is like the wise man?
And who knows the interpretation of a thing?
Wisdom makes one's face shine,
and the hardness of one's countenance is changed.
—Ecclesiastes 8:1

In the book of Ecclesiastes, God does not speak. That is, the divine voice is not quoted. God does not answer. In other books of the Bible, even when the theme of hiddenness asserts itself, God eventually reveals God's message. Indeed God's voice booms elsewhere in the scriptures; it initiates, creates, instructs, corrects, answers. In the book of Genesis God speaks the universe into being. In the Psalms God counsels, soothes, demands. In the book of Job God thunders from out of the whirlwind to the dissident malcontent. As recorded through prophets and other chosen human vessels, God's voice delivers news, annunciations, world-quaking revelations.

But in Ecclesiastes God does not speak. What to make of this? The ancient rabbis fretted over this divine silence. Some argued that Ecclesiastes was not worthy of inclusion in holy scripture; the absence of God's direct words only reinforced that point. What is God's attitude toward Ecclesiastes? Does God endorse this book?

The debate continued on into the first century CE until it was finally settled. Ultimately Ecclesiastes was accepted as part of the canon of scripture, partly because of the book's association with Solomon, partly too because there were enough pious passages (put there by a watchful editor?) to give it a sheen of orthodoxy.

God's silence in the book of Ecclesiastes may strike the reader even now as puzzling or ominous. Yet if you believe everything in scripture is there for a purpose, then Ecclesiastes' strange presence has its own irresistible reasons and urgency.

In the Bible Ecclesiastes serves as a place of refuge for a particular moment in the spiritual life—a time of trouble, dismay, and recovery, whether the reader is a lone individual or a standing-room-only congregation or a soul-searching nation. Ecclesiastes is the book for times when God does not answer in the expected way. Ecclesiastes is like a rocky isle on the map of Bible reading—a windswept place, hard to reach, yet nevertheless a place to land and hear things said that no one else says in scripture or in modern spiritual America.

Ecclesiastes is not so isolated from the rest of scripture after all. He enshrines a human condition that is blessed elsewhere—the "poor in spirit," those who feel silenced by defeat or depleted by family trouble or who hold on to faith despite the overwhelming arid desert winds. They wait while aggressors and predators sow confusion at center stage, using God's name in vain to endorse their own self-serving ideologies or self-pity—terrorists who murder to please God, racists who quote God's Word to justify bigotry, politicians who call on the Lord while carousing with dictators and cutting off public aid to poor children. "Blessed are the poor in spirit," Jesus taught—those who lack the spiritual vocabulary of boasting, with no access to prime-time power or media, and no inclination to smooth over the hard times with rosy talk.

In this first verse of chapter 8, Ecclesiastes is again preoccupied with wisdom. The subject of wisdom may hold a clue to one of the Bible's enduring enigmas. Commentators have noted a strange phenomenon in scripture: in the Hebrew Bible, God "disappears" after the divine whirlwind appearance at the end of the book of Job. God stops speaking directly. After Job, God speaks through prophets and other seers, but not in dramatic, personal divine epiphanies. This gradual withdrawal in the Old Testament has been mapped by scholar Richard Elliott Friedman this way:

Moses glimpses the divine at Sinai. But the last time God is said to be "revealed" to a human is to the prophet Samuel. The last public miracle is the divine fire for Elijah at Mount Carmel. The last personal miracle is when the shadow reverses before Isaiah and Hezekiah.[1]

Some explain this slow divine withdrawal as God's own discouragement at the folly and fecklessness of human beings; God withdraws in grief.

But there's another way to look at it: God gradually gives humans more and more responsibility to live out God's purposes on their own. God reveals the divine laws, and humans slowly and despite many false steps write God's purposes on their hearts. Miracles give way to maturity. The spirit of God becomes housed in words. Wisdom is one such house of words. The Bible's wisdom literature, including Ecclesiastes, can be seen as a later depository of God's expectations, built on the shoulders of the story of God's relationship with ancient Israel but now moving ahead without the aid, or the crutch, of God's overwhelming personal interventions.

Wisdom was a new way for God to interact with people. Wisdom made it possible for people to internalize God's spirit and purposes. Wisdom was God's method of entrusting us with the freedom to do the right thing. Ecclesiastes becomes another of God's unlikely deputies, witnessing to the faith lived out in battle conditions of doubt, half-blindness, and breakthrough.

Wisdom "makes one's face shine," the sage says. This has echoes in Numbers 6:25, where God says to Moses, "The LORD make his face to shine upon you, and be gracious to you." Such radiance, in scripture, signals divine blessing and favor. God may be silent in Ecclesiastes, but a divine glow burns through nevertheless.

Keep the king's command because of your sacred oath. Do not be terrified; go from his presence, do not delay when the matter is unpleasant, for he does whatever he pleases. For the word of the king is powerful, and who can say to him, "What are you doing?" Whoever obeys a command will meet no harm, and the wise mind will know the time and way. For every matter has its time and way, although the troubles of mortals lie heavy upon them. Indeed, they do not know what is to be, for who can tell them how it will be? No one has power over the wind to restrain the wind, or power over the day of death; there is no discharge from the battle, nor does wickedness deliver those who practice it. All this I observed, applying my mind to all that is done under the sun, while one person exercises authority over another to the other's hurt. (8:2-9)

I've never met a king. There are fewer and fewer of them these days to meet. I know people who have met the queen of England and the pope, but I haven't had the pleasure. I did meet a president once, Jimmy Carter, just a handshake on the crowded campaign trail. The experience lasted two seconds, but I still recall it thirty years later. He was a serious, soft-spoken man of faith. Too soft-spoken— he lost reelection. After Carter, voters decided to put more swagger in the Oval Office, electing men who believe in God all right but who'll go to war for the American way of life and never apologize.

Chances are, Ecclesiastes never met a king either. The time of Hebrew kings had passed. Political defeats and captivities took care of that. There hadn't been a real Hebrew king for nearly three hundred years. The closest king in his time, if Ecclesiastes was writing about 250 BCE, would have been some three hundred miles to the west in Alexandria, King Ptolemy. Nevertheless, Ecclesiastes knew what everyone knew: monarchs demanded absolute power and claimed the favor of God. Ecclesiastes appears to be familiar with court protocol, etiquette, and political psychology. So here we perhaps get a glimpse of Ecclesiastes' daily work as a teacher. He offers practical advice, probably to elite groups of young men who one day might seek vocational work in a royal court or foreign service.[2]

But Ecclesiastes adds a twist. Instead of fawning and kissing up to power, he injects some skepticism into his instructions. He cuts the kings down to human size by noting the obvious: even kings don't know how things will turn out; only God knows. Kings enjoy taking on the trappings of the divine, but that usually guarantees a legacy of excess, overextension, then military disaster. And people suffer. Ecclesiastes possibly had in mind the history of his own people, most recently a luckless king like Zedekiah, who came to the throne under the thumb of the Babylonians in the sixth century BCE. Zedekiah ignored the warnings of the prophet Jeremiah and recklessly decided to revolt against the hated foreign rulers. His rebellion was crushed. The enemy Babylon laid siege to Jerusalem and destroyed it. Zedekiah was caught in Jericho. His army deserted him. The description of his torture, in 2 Kings, still causes a shudder. His sons were slaughtered in his presence, then his eyes were put out, and he was led off to Babylon in chains, the last king of Judah (2 Kings 25:5-7).

"No one has power over the wind to restrain the wind, or power over the day of death," Ecclesiastes warned his pupils. This is the heart of the matter. God withholds information from us, for God's own reasons. No political leader can afford to admit this. The ruler's instinct is always to look confident, work in secret, underestimate resistance, and deny unpredictability. But in our tabloid world of instant video, news leaks, and Internet rumor, secrets are hard to keep, outcomes difficult to control. Dictators, kings, and presidents find it harder and harder to govern restless majorities, solve poverty, stop extremism, or run a war.

We're in the middle of war ourselves, whether it's called a war against terror or a struggle for Mideast stability and world oil. The stakes and rhetoric rise to biblical proportions, destination unknown. Our job is to stay alert, have a Plan B, and pay attention to the prophets in our midst.

Ecclesiastes as good as warned us.

Then I saw the wicked buried; they used to go in and out of the holy place, and were praised in the city where they had done such things. This also is vanity. Because sentence against an evil deed is not executed speedily, the human heart is fully set to do evil. Though sinners do evil a hundred times and prolong their lives, yet I know that it will be well with those who fear God, because they stand in fear before him, but it will not be well with the wicked, neither will they prolong their days like a shadow, because they do not stand in fear before God. (8:10-13)

In the twenty-first century, evil is making a comeback. Not since Hitler has evil been so personified as the way we have conferred it on terrorism. Not since the Civil War have our leaders and pundits become such eager armchair theologians, urging us to fight the good fight against evil.

This baffles the sociologists who, in the wild, naive 1960s, had predicted the death of religion. Such was the childlike faith of secular optimism—the belief that humankind would emancipate itself from all traditional authorities and finally attain the brilliance of rational enlightenment.

Instead, of course, the new millennium arrived awash in religion —high levels of religious affiliation in the United States, the spread of world Pentecostalism, fascination with spiritual best-sellers, the countless charitable initiatives—but also a dark side, religious anger virtually medieval in intensity, issuing forth in video beheadings, car bombs, bloody civil wars.

More bad news for the baffled sociologists: the only remedy for bad religion is more religion—namely, a healthy fear of God, as Ecclesiastes would say. Fear of God means commitment to God's purposes, hand in hand with a deep wariness of the human capacity for evil.

War complicates and muddies the picture. "The human heart is fully set to do evil," Ecclesiastes says. Not just the enemy's heart, not just other people's. Everybody's heart. My heart. In war time the temptation is to make exceptions. Close ranks, lest the enemy exploit our self-doubts. Choke dissent, lest some people appear unpatriotic. Evil is limited to the scowling face of the enemy. Self-searching humility gets brushed aside. With military might we're making sure we're putting the fear of God in others.

"Fear of God" may be the simplest phrase in scripture—and the hardest.

> There is a vanity that takes place on earth, that there are right-eous people who are treated according to the conduct of the wicked, and there are wicked people who are treated according to the conduct of the righteous. I said that this also is vanity. So I commend enjoyment, for there is nothing better for people under the sun than to eat, and drink, and enjoy themselves, for this will go with them in their toil through the days of life that God gives them under the sun. (8:14-15)

Enjoy. Seven times Ecclesiastes urges this in his book. It's part of his wisdom strategy, a gravitational force, his advice for grabbing the present moment before it gets away.

"Eat, drink, and enjoy . . ." This is the serene, unexpected face of religion. In my experience, the ways of faith are far more contentious and competitive. Time after time, conflict is far more energizing than a theological affirmation such as the goodness of the senses. Sectarian doctrine feeds the need to argue, the need to win the debate, get the last word. Historically this characterized the free-market spread of faith across the American frontier—competition, conflict, doctrinal scrimmaging. The style is as vibrant today as two hundred years ago. In conversations and confrontations, a harsh logic kicks in. Believing in God is not enough. One must be, say, a Christian. Being a Christian isn't enough. One must be a certain kind of Christian, the right denomination with the right credentials. Being the right kind of churchgoer isn't enough. You have to have the right view of atonement or homosexuality or the timing of the Rapture.

In a marketplace milieu, the pressure is constant to wander away from the spirit of biblical wisdom and good sense. Fear takes over, an addiction to argument, being on the winning side. There's an itch for mastery over the chaos. Everybody wants mastery. Fashion, money, power, perfectionism—not just religious debate—are all about mastery. Driving a huge gas-guzzler is an attempt at mastery, an attempt to feel safe and intimidating on the road. Instead, such cars are slaves to oil consumption and high gas prices; also they're dangerous to drive. Workaholism is an attempt at mastery. But it ends in disappointment, ill health, a stingy view of life and love. Lottery players attempt mastery, but they are pawns of public policy, transferring money from the poor to the rich.

It's tempting to try to master even God, insisting God is on our team, working for my agenda, submitting to my needs—God the local god or the national deity—in order to ease fears of the future or of other people.

In Ecclesiastes' world, wisdom springs not from fear of life but awe of God. The declaration "All is vanity" has a practical use: it frees the mind from excessive material attachments, the need for more, the fear of never possessing them, the fear of losing them, the fear that they will not make us happy after all. God gives people the capacity to discover truths and live them. And even enjoy them. This is mastery of the present moment—and, paradoxically, submission to the moment.

> When I applied my mind to know wisdom, and to see the business that is done on earth, how one's eyes see sleep neither day nor night, then I saw all the work of God, that no one can find out what is happening under the sun. However much they may toil in seeking, they will not find it out; even though those who are wise claim to know, they cannot find it out. (8:16-17)

Is Ecclesiastes the strangest book in the Bible? One other book might compete for the title—the book of Revelation at the end of the New Testament. Revelation may be the most quoted and least read book in scripture, full of florid imagery of God's future judgment, the sufferings to come, the glories that Jesus will establish, the new Jerusalem and new earth.

The book of Revelation is promoted as the great arsenal of apocalypse. Lately it has been ransacked to provide plot points for the rising genre of frightening movies and novels that warn in scary detail about the end times. Lost in the noise are the levelheaded surmises of mainstream scholars, who long ago concluded that Revelation is a visionary book encapsulating the fears and hopes of first-century Christians undergoing persecution in Rome—not a detailed blueprint for twenty-first-century Armageddon.

Besides strangeness, Revelation and Ecclesiastes have this in common: both were late entries into the biblical canon. In the case of Revelation, some Christians refused to accept it into their Bible for four hundred years. Its authorship was uncertain, its imagery jarring and out of sync with the rest of the New Testament.

Otherwise Ecclesiastes stands opposite to Revelation in most every other regard. Ecclesiastes does assume the future judgment of God—he says so. But he refuses to speculate the details. He refuses to unleash scenarios of future cataclysm and consummation. By abstaining, by holding his cards close, Ecclesiastes left no quotable legacy of misunderstanding. He offered no apocalyptic material that could be exploited or abused for purposes of spiritual manipulation or fraud. He never played into the history of false warnings that have confused and disillusioned so many generations who put their trust in overzealous peddlers of doom, embroidered by misuses of the book of Revelation.

It's as if Ecclesiastes anticipated Jesus by 250 years—the Jesus who said he would return but warned against idle speculation about things that only God can know, like the timing of the last days and final judgment (Matt. 24:34-36 and Mark 13:30-32).

Ecclesiastes put it his own way in his own time: "However much they may toil in seeking, they will not find it out" (8:17). The world would be a less anxious place if his words had found their way long ago into humanity's troubled religious imagination.

CHAPTER 9
GOD'S FINGERPRINTS

> All this I laid to heart, examining it all, how the righteous and the wise and their deeds are in the hand of God; whether it is love or hate one does not know. Everything that confronts them is vanity, since the same fate comes to all, to the righteous and the wicked, to the good and the evil, to the clean and the unclean, to those who sacrifice and those who do not sacrifice. As are the good, so are the sinners; those who swear are like those who shun an oath.
>
> —Ecclesiastes 9:1-2

A church marquee caught my eye the other day: "Coincidence is God's way of staying anonymous." That one's worth a whole book, a congressional inquiry, a national referendum.

Coincidence hints at divine intersection in everyday routine and cosmic secrets disclosed. "It's a God thing," people say when seemingly random events result in a great new job or a narrow brush with death unscathed. Scrutiny of coincidence was big after 9/11—all the stories about people who were delayed in traffic or who called in sick and so didn't get on the ill-fated planes or get to work on time at the World Trade Center, and were spared. We peer deep into coincidences to crack their meaning, half expecting light to stream out of them, the light that will illuminate why we're still here and others are not.

Ecclesiastes scans the range of human experience and declares it's all "in the hand of God." That's where we are—in the hands of providence. As Jesus put it, God counts every hair on your head; everything's in God's hands, not ours, so be not anxious.

Ecclesiastes and Jesus speak the same truth: God's in control; I'm not. Jesus points to the flourishing lilies and the well-fed birds as reassuring signs of God's detailed attention. Ecclesiastes looks to other basic elements of divine sustenance—the ground under our feet, the capacity to enjoy the good earth. There's plenty of work to do: follow the commandments; remember the awe of God in daily life. Jesus boiled it down to love of God and neighbor.

I think of Ecclesiastes as a literalist who allowed himself only a few things to believe in, the things God gave him to know. One of them is this: The earth is a literal miracle of God. It was conceived and created. It has a history and a beginning. It was once not here. It did not have to exist. It arrived at the pleasure of the Creator, a crossroads of creation, where encounters happen between mortals and the divine. It's where the story of redemption unfolds.

Another literal miracle: the notion of eternity stamped on our minds. Some call it soul, or the image of God, or the kingdom of God within, or the unique ability of humans to imagine their own death, their own life after death. This is God's touch on the human species.

These are the miraculous materials Ecclesiastes keeps in mind as he muses over and over about providence, that most confounding idea of all. He jousts with it, broods about its motions, its wheels and inner workings. It's an overwhelming concept, scattering theologians in a dozen directions. It's hard to mention providence at all without deleting human beings as a factor in the scheme of things. If providence exists—if God's will shapes all that happens—then what role do people have? Does free will exist?

The Bible is not an encyclopedia that gives an elaborate textbook definition of providence. But the basic lines are set down: providence means God sees the end from the beginning. Providence means God has a plan; providence is the will of the Almighty, who is "actively involved in moving his creation to a goal."[1] Nothing happens without a reason. History is not cyclical or meaningless, though from the human point of view it can look chaotic and random. In the Bible, the Creator God personally regulates the created world but includes us in the game plan. Our choices become part of the story. In the Christian view, God intensified the meaning of providence by entering human life in the form of Jesus of Nazareth, penetrating history in a decisive new way and guaranteeing that God's providential goal of salvation is on course to the end.

The question of providence haunts daily life now as much as ever. Christians and non-Christians look for providential meaning in every pivotal personal surprise or strange coincidence—Did I fall into this career, or did God arrange it? Did you win the lottery because God said so? Does God bless America? Is providence the reason those people died in the car wreck and I didn't? Ecclesiastes' phrase "the hand of God" looms large and enigmatic.

But providence has competition these days. Luck is a major rival to providence in a nation where almost every state now has legalized gambling. People buy lottery tickets to make their own luck, write their own script of destiny. Luck elbows in on providence as the way more and more people explain their world.

The other big rival is technology. Every day the media bring news of the latest feats of gene splicing, "smart" missiles, and wireless gadgets. It's tempting to conclude I alone control my own destiny if I have the right tech support; providence is dispensable. Scientists talk now of the day when some lucky future generation will overcome mortality itself (that is, those citizens who have the money to buy immortality by affording a permanent regimen of organ transplants).

I will stick with providence and live with the paradoxes. Here's one: I believe in providence as long as I don't dwell too much on its details or demand to know how it works. Obsessing about it, a person veers in the direction of bossy, self-serving claims to know the will of God about everything. Or careens down the opposite path of despair, disbelief, and fatalism, losing hope in human ability to do anything worthwhile, or dismissing the whole thing; God's fingerprints are nowhere.

The book of Ecclesiastes does not despair as long as wisdom, awe, and wonder stay within reach. They're available to everybody. Paradoxes are built into the system. Deny them, and you let go of the hand of God.

> This is an evil in all that happens under the sun, that the same fate comes to everyone. Moreover, the hearts of all are full of evil; madness is in their hearts while they live, and after that they go to the dead. But whoever is joined with all the living has hope, for a living dog is better than a dead lion. The living know that they will die, but the dead know nothing; they have no more reward, and even the memory of them is lost. (9:3-5)

Death is the end, Ecclesiastes says. Christianity disagrees, saying there is no end. Death is defeated. Jesus' resurrection assures us the prospect of an afterlife in the glory of God. But practically speaking, we are not so far away from Ecclesiastes' situation. Christian doctrine doesn't stop anyone from anxious day-to-day musings about death, the unpredictable certainty. Christianity itself is not of one mind about the details of the afterlife or the nature of what awaits. Are people immediately dispatched at death to heaven and hell? Or does everyone's soul wait in gravelike repose until the Last Judgment? Both beliefs are found in Christian teaching.

Ecclesiastes, writing perhaps 250 years before Jesus' birth, contends with the question according to the terms of his own era. The matter raged with controversy.

Why death? The answer evolves throughout the pages of scripture. The book of Genesis lays out the story of death in the beginning. It is punishment against Adam and Eve for disobeying God.

The traditional Hebrew view emerged: death ended for everybody in *Sheol,* a word that shows up sixty-five times in the Old Testament. It meant not extinction but a shadowy afterlife in the underworld, the pit, a place removed from God's care. The devout dreaded it for that reason: it separated them from God.

But scripture doesn't contain many details about Sheol. Did people in Sheol remain conscious? Over time, speculation grew impatient with Sheol's bland finality. By Ecclesiastes' day, new thoughts were influencing ideas about death and pushing Sheol out of the picture.

One was the Greek idea of the immortal soul, a notion seeping into Israelite society since the invasion of Alexander the Great.

Another idea erupted out of the anguished experience of Jewish persecution and martyrdom. People were being killed defending the Torah against its enemies. What happens to them at death? Surely God would never dispatch his courageous loyalists to shadowy Sheol. Shouldn't something better await the martyrs of the Lord?

This thought was pushed further. Surely God wouldn't have gone to the trouble of forming a covenant with his people only to allow the relationship to be cut off forever at death. The sheer logic of faith and the pressures of history challenged tradition's definition of Sheol.

In the Psalms sweaty prayers about death were always near. Psalm 139 insists the sovereign God is bigger than death, so nothing shall separate the Lord from God's creatures, not even Sheol.

Ecclesiastes remains unmoved. "The dead know nothing," he says. Sheol was an unconscious state. His words defy the new intellectual trends that were overwhelming the scene. Some say he displayed the stubborn resistance of a religious conservative, evidence that he came from the patrician ranks of Israelite society. Whatever his reasons, instead of pouring energy into scenarios of afterlife, Ecclesiastes saves his affection for the meaning of living. When we die, no matter what awaits, this earthly life of wonders and pleasures and perplexities ceases. Ecclesiastes refuses to sugarcoat it. He urges action—*carpe diem*, "seize the day." *Carpe diem* has Latin pagan origins (from poet Horace): eat, drink, be merry; tomorrow I might keel over. But Ecclesiastes revises the credo. He adds this: and remember God, for God has granted it all.

Their love and their hate and their envy have already perished; never again will they have any share in all that happens under the sun.

Go, eat your bread with enjoyment, and drink your wine with a merry heart; for God has long ago approved what you do. (9:6-7)

Back in the mid-1970s, the Paul Simon song "Slip Slidin' Away" was big on the radio. I remember being stuck in traffic on the interstate, a twenty-year-old heading back to college after the holidays, anxious about exams, career, the future. The song was playing on the AM dial, and suddenly the lyrics entered deep into my bones: God has a plan, Simon crooned, but "the information's unavailable to the mortal man."

I had not heard anyone say it so plainly. The friendly bluntness of his statement struck me not as despair but a kind of blessing, a way forward—trust life, trust the plan, whether I had access to it or not.

When I eventually read Ecclesiastes I saw that he was working the same territory, with this twist: he wasn't a twenty-something in the grip of anxiety but an elder looking back on his life, a life of experimentation and false trails and wise assessments. He knew what later Christian philosopher Søren Kierkegaard knew: Life must be lived forward but is understood backward. Only later can you see the arc of your life, the story it became, all the decisions—good and bad—that add up to who you are.

Sitting there, miserably stuck in traffic in an aging AMC Gremlin, smack in the middle of the storm of youth, I didn't know how my life's story would possibly unfold. Campus preachers were telling me everything is preordained by God. Maybe so, but the concept wasn't doing me much good; I still had to make decisions without any inkling of any preordained anything. Nearly thirty years later, the story is more than half finished; twenty-something anxieties are replaced by forty-something anxieties, but the story is finally making sense.

Ecclesiastes boldly says, "Go, eat your bread with enjoyment, and drink your wine with a merry heart; for God has long ago approved what you do." Some hastily call this despair. Others dare to call it life.

Let your garments always be white; do not let oil be lacking on your head. Enjoy life with the wife whom you love, all the days of your vain life that are given you under the sun, because that is your portion in life and in your toil at which you toil under the sun. Whatever your hand finds to do, do with your might; for there is no work or thought or knowledge or wisdom in Sheol, to which you are going. (9:8-10)

Ecclesiastes preaches now, fierce and direct. But I resist his Sheol. We've inherited a vastly different set of expectations and intellectual coordinates, twenty-three hundred years later—a Christian culture whose central story for two millennia has been the Resurrection of Jesus and an eternal afterlife of paradise or regret awaiting all.

It raises a new question, one of the great what-ifs of spiritual history: If Ecclesiastes had believed in a more vivid afterlife—if he had lived later and been a Christian believer in the Resurrection—would his message be different? Would he say all is vanity? Would he urge readers to enjoy this life with such insistence?

But wait. Those questions assume the cliché that a Christian hope of the afterlife means discounting the pleasures of this life. It's a grim puritan vestige, a spiritual distortion of a legitimate conviction: Life is serious and the stakes are high. One's eternal soul hangs in the balance.

Even if Ecclesiastes were Christian, I picture him going about his ethical teaching in much the same way he always did. Fear God; follow the commandments; be grateful—these ideas are compatible with Christianity already.

The challenge boomerangs back at us. How should believers in the Resurrection conduct themselves? Some live out the answer with kindness, patience, a sense of humor, and self-forgetful sacrifice. Others nurture an all-consuming resentment of the wider culture, a crusade of negativism, a persecution complex. The world looks on, puzzled by this inconsistent witness. A little Ecclesiastes in the diet might do everybody some good.

Again I saw that under the sun the race is not to the swift, nor the battle to the strong, nor bread to the wise, nor riches to the intelligent, nor favor to the skillful; but time and chance happen to them all. For no one can anticipate the time of disaster. Like fish taken in a cruel net, and like birds caught in a snare, so mortals are snared at a time of calamity, when it suddenly falls upon them. (9:11-12)

Did Ecclesiastes pray? In "the time of calamity," did he petition the Lord? What would he ask of God? Or did he consider it "vain" to pray? He says we cannot know the divine mind or manipulate the divine will. So is it pointless to pray?

I don't find evidence that he rejected prayer—not if God is the all-knowing sovereign Lord, as Ecclesiastes acknowledges. Nevertheless, it's hard to imagine a greater clash of spiritual styles than that of Ecclesiastes and the surging trends of today. What would he make of sermons that promise God will reward you with undreamed-of material rewards (bigger house, better job, more of everything good) if you pray fervently and tithe? What would he say to the Spirit-filled excitements of a healing service?

I've been to such services, large and small. I recall one in particular. Toward the end, the minister invited everyone to come up and be touched for a healing. The thirty worshipers lined up and, one by one, each fell gently to the floor after the minister's touch on the forehead. Soon the whole church was eerily silent—everyone was stretched out in the aisles, under the pews, perfectly still. I was with a photographer, who viewed the scene with alarm. He wanted to call 911. I assured him all was well, then stepped carefully over several people in order to talk to the minister, who was out of breath at the wonders of God. After twenty minutes people slowly got up, a bit dazed, and went home. There was no concluding blessing or organ postlude. Several people would return that same night for another round of miracles.

This happens every day now all over the world, the barnstorming spread of Christian Pentecostalism. The words of Ecclesiastes are very far from such moments. It is odd that the Bible should contain such wildly different messages—here, Ecclesiastes' discouragement about the world's possibilities; elsewhere, a son is born to the elderly Abraham and Sarah, and later the Son of God is born to Mary. It's tempting to say our latter-day theologies of positive thinking and church marketing render Ecclesiastes void, obsolete. But this is not what centuries of biblical belief say. The Bible is one unified document. Paradoxically, the sheer diversity of scripture's moods and circumstances gives it authority. The Bible's many witnesses—the Psalms, Job, Jeremiah, the cries of Jesus on the cross—

cover the difficult spectrum of human feeling and resonate with the world of the reader, says scholar Phyllis Trible.[3] Each book of the Bible is a chapter in the history of human destiny and divine appointment. Each adds to the picture.

Ecclesiastes is a realist whose instincts never leave him. When the spiritual carnival of optimism has the floor, the world's tragedies go unmentioned—no reference to hurricane deaths or friendly fire or spinal meningitis or the pink mist of the World Trade Center slaughter. News of the human condition itself is suspended. History is whited out. Ecclesiastes arrives to say human life is also defined by other spiritual moods that visit without an invitation—seasons of waiting for God's answer, feelings of absence or frustration, moments of hard-won contentment in the silence.

But I still think Ecclesiastes prayed.

I have also seen this example of wisdom under the sun, and it seemed great to me. There was a little city with few people in it. A great king came against it and besieged it, building great siege-works against it. Now there was found in it a poor wise man, and he by his wisdom delivered the city. Yet no one remembered that poor man. So I said, "Wisdom is better than might; yet the poor man's wisdom is despised, and his words are not heeded."

The quiet words of the wise are more to be heeded than the shouting of a ruler among fools.

Wisdom is better than weapons of war but one bungler destroys much good. (9:13-18)

In the old days, two topics were forbidden in polite conversation: religion and politics. Now they dominate. God is entangled in geopolitical headlines and election returns. Spiritualized politics and politicized religion cheapen the name of God and take it in vain. Every ideological position claims God on its side, presuming God's future blessing. But Ecclesiastes embarrasses everybody, saying God has blocked mortals from finding out "anything that will come after them" (7:14).

Still, it's hard to read the Bible without thinking of current events, even if scripture gets enlisted as a mere tool of left- or right-wing purposes. This puzzling passage invites furious discussion about wisdom and politics and how they often repel each other. How can we sort out our many versions of national identity? We're a religious nation that looks to the Bible for personal morality. We're a secular nation that separates church from state and looks to eighteenth-century Enlightenment ideas of civil life. We believe in optimism—and original sin. Many embrace faith in humanistic progress, an unstoppable future of improvement—or an imminent apocalypse where God's judgment will overwhelm the earth and begin a new reign of heavenly glory. Bibles sell big. Guns sell big. Which is the real American story?

An argument can be made that we're in the middle of a historic spiritual revival, maybe a new Great Awakening. Megachurches thrive. Religious best-sellers trigger national conversation. Born-again Christian voters flex political muscle. Alternative spiritualities abound. Does it all add up to a nation transformed? What would a real revival look like? What *should* it look like? Are ethics and decency on the rise? No statistics suggest cheating is in decline or that violence and pornography are in a slump. Is an epidemic of compassion on the loose, here and abroad? "The quiet words of the wise man are more to be heeded than the shouting of a ruler among fools," Ecclesiastes says. Is the Bible read more closely than ever, or is it skimmed and left behind?

Biblical wisdom seems to mean two things—suspicion of human corruptible power and yet the need to use human power to spread compassion. Ecclesiastes insists wisdom is better than might, better than weapons of war.

My idea of a reformation would include a fearless wrestle with Ecclesiastes' challenge. Emotionally engaging his words—even with anger or embarrassment—would be a first sign of hope.

CHAPTER 10
ELECTION DAY

Dead flies make the perfumer's ointment give off a foul odor;
so a little folly outweighs wisdom and honor.
The heart of the wise inclines to the right,
but the heart of a fool to the left.
Even when fools walk on the road, they lack sense,
and show to everyone that they are fools.
—Ecclesiastes 10:1-3

Last night I was reading Ecclesiastes in the Bible my church gave me forty years ago when I was seven. It's a modest, wonderful Bible—thin black leather, with photos and maps but shyly without commentary and notes, just the scripture delivered straight, an edition still standing at attention after four decades, its white onionskin pages in good shape, holding back the mustiness of the passing years, a Bible as readable as the day I received it as a confirmation gift in August 1964. "Holy Bible" it says on the cover, matter-of-factly.

I remember the moment at the altar rail. It occurred in a large Methodist sanctuary, a big-boned building in a transitional urban neighborhood (it still is). The minister asked us kids to take up the Bible's challenge and read it with heart and concentration, and act upon it. No one got in my face about what to read or how to interpret it. The adults told us the Bible was true, and we would find that out for ourselves if we read it faithfully and kept our eyes open to the blessings of God. Presumably they knew Ecclesiastes was in there too, with its sobering thoughts and chilling words. But they did not rip it out of the scriptures or warn me about its contents.

I didn't know that night that I carried my new Bible into a world on the edge of convulsion, and fast coming. The list of social tumult is familiar now, of course: Vietnam, civil rights, sexual revolution, the Beatles and Rolling Stones, the erosion of every sort of authority. The religious upheavals of that time still play out today—the declining power of mainline churches, the spread of non-aligned megachurches, the proliferation of non-Christian faiths, the popularity of do-it-yourself spirituality, and the emergence of evangelical Protestants as a powerfully self-conscious voting bloc and consumer category. Interest in spirituality is up, yet church affiliation is falling.

Ironically, the more spiritual America gets, the less influence the Bible appears to have. The hundreds of translations and editions of scripture today—jazzed up or dumbed down—speak to the fretful assumption that consumers are harder and harder to reach. The first rule of church marketing now is this: Don't assume visitors know anything about faith or scripture. And don't talk churchy. Ministers have to spend more and more pulpit time on the mere rudiments of the sacred stories. The Bible has its public defenders who call it America's foundational document and God's last stand in an era of moral chaos, pluralism, and decadent pop culture. But it's not obvious who's reading the big sections—the Torah, the Prophets, the sayings of Jesus. If Bible reading declines, ideas about the Almighty will be shaped by pop trends and consumer expectations. God comes off as a house deity working for the home team. Awe becomes an alien concept. Religion becomes another commodity, reinforcing politics, making no threat to economic consumption patterns. In a nation that's 85 percent Christian, a vast national debate about war in Iraq can proceed for months without any public figure quoting Jesus' troublesome blessings on the peacemakers in the Sermon on the Mount or Ecclesiastes' warnings about human vanity and the travails of the poor. Instead, the Bible is enlisted as a trump-card weapon in a permanent culture war, where scripture is quoted in micropassages to support arguments on a rotating list of hot-button issues—usually homosexuality, Hollywood, and prayer in school.

Scripture will outlast every foolish abuse. Forty years pass, and I'm reading Ecclesiastes' chapter 10, a group of proverbs on the give-and-take of wisdom and folly. Somehow those Methodist adults who gave us the Bible trusted us kids with its contents. They entrusted its future to us, trusting life to deliver its moments to us one by one, with scripture nearby, revealing beams of light one by one, no longer hidden or embedded. My church never gave us marching orders regarding the inspiration of scripture. We would discover that idea for ourselves. What made the Bible sacred to me was the grandeur and strangeness of its stories and personalities, too strange to make up, sealed originally in those Hebrew and Greek letters, and its way of speaking to daily circumstances, its bloom in the heart. Even in years when I neglected it, the authority of the Bible never diminished. I felt diminished by ignoring it.

The wind blows where it will, said Jesus, and indeed said Ecclesiastes. Life piles up. Death piles up—loved ones, parents of friends, friends. The circle closes in a little tighter every year. Life seems determined to break every heart. Ecclesiastes speaks; the Gospels and prophets speak. When they handed me the Bible that night, they were helping us all pack for a long road ahead.

If the anger of the ruler rises against you,
do not leave your post,
for calmness will undo great offenses.
There is an evil that I have seen under the sun, as great an error
as if it proceeded from the ruler: folly is set in many high
places, and the rich sit in a low place. I have seen slaves on
horseback, and princes walking on foot like slaves.
Whoever digs a pit will fall into it;
and whoever breaks through a wall will be bitten by a snake.
Whoever quarries stones will be hurt by them;
and whoever splits logs will be endangered by them.
If the iron is blunt, and one does not whet the edge,

then more strength must be exerted;
but wisdom helps one to succeed.
If the snake bites before it is charmed,
there is no advantage in a charmer. (10:4-11)

We come to a pothole on the journey through Ecclesiastes. Chapter 10 rides like a clunky, clanging jalopy. Perhaps the editing of Ecclesiastes' teachings broke down in this chapter. The enduring mystery about Ecclesiastes is how it came to be written. Does the book, as a whole, make sense or not? Is it incoherent or does it have a finely wrought structure? Was it composed by one writer or a dozen? Did Ecclesiastes sit down to write, or dictate it to students, or leave a stack of notes for them to decipher and compile? Is it a complete, intact book or a ragged first draft with holes to fill? Some defend the book as a record of the evolving thoughts of one man getting older and older. Or did an editor swoop in and save Ecclesiastes from obscurity by sprucing it up, adding enough references to God and the commandments to make the book more attractive to the overseers of the scriptural canon? If so, this presumably careful editor skipped over whole portions that could have used clarifying. Chapter 10 includes passages, like this one at first reading, that look tacked on or too general to leave much of an impression.

But in the details it's possible to see hints about the stressed-out, practical lives of Ecclesiastes' first audiences. Chapter 10 is laced with menace, images of danger and risk. Scholar C. L. Seow argues that Ecclesiastes is speaking sensibly and directly to the anxious economic roller coaster of Israel under Persian, then Greek, dominance.[1] The economy was fast-paced. There was money to be made. Minted coinage became widespread under Persian influence after the sixth century BCE. The result? A climate of entrepreneurship, business risk, and annual taxation. People faced the prospect of fortunes gained and lost overnight, with business opportunities in livestock, farming, an array of urban shopkeeping and real-estate ventures. Slaves (or former slaves) could become rich by subleasing land to other slaves. But investment and borrowing were expensive. Risk, debt, and foreclosures ran deep. The politics of the region added to the uncertainty as foreign powers vied for the upper hand in the Holy Land. People overworked themselves out of worry about slipping into poverty, Seow says. All this Ecclesiastes kept in mind as he painted a picture of a precarious world of politics and finance easily toppled and turned on its head, with snares and pits at every turn.

If this sounds a bit familiar, like a twenty-first-century scenario of high-octane opportunities and vulnerable markets and mounting incidence of personal and national debt and uncertain politics, then it's neither the first time nor the last that the elusive Ecclesiastes manages to slip past the gatekeeping editors and whisper into our ear.

> Words spoken by the wise bring them favor,
> but the lips of fools consume them.
> The words of their mouths begin in foolishness,
> and their talk ends in wicked madness;
> yet fools talk on and on.
> No one knows what is to happen,
> and who can tell anyone what the future holds?
> The toil of fools wears them out,
> for they do not even know the way to town. (10:12-15)

If Ecclesiastes isn't puzzling enough, his book is sometimes mistaken for two other texts of wisdom writing from biblical times, further confusing the picture. They are Ecclesiasticus (also known as The Wisdom of Jesus Son of Sirach) and The Wisdom of Solomon.

Both of these books are in Catholic Bibles but not Protestant or Jewish Bibles. In Catholic scriptures they belong to the deutero-canonical writings, or "second canon" writings, because they were written later than the established books of the Old Testament, though they are still considered important religious works. Neither of them, however, was included in the Hebrew Bible that the Jewish authorities assembled in the first century CE. Instead they were grouped with writings known as the Apocrypha. The Protestants took their lead from the Hebrew Bible and kept Ecclesiasticus and Wisdom of Solomon out of the primary canonical Bible but included them as Apocrypha worthy of study.

Ecclesiasticus (or Sirach), written perhaps one hundred years after Ecclesiastes, is one of the longest sacred books associated with the Bible. It was written by a well-traveled Jewish teacher named Jesus Son of Sirach, who was steeped in Greek culture but determined to demonstrate the vigor and relevance of traditional Jewish thought in his changing times. He probably wrote the book in Hebrew around 180 BCE, then his grandson translated it into Greek around 132 BCE. Its fifty-one wide-ranging chapters include autobiographical details, proverbs on duty to parents, and praise for Lady Wisdom: "Those who obey her will judge the nations, and all who listen to her will live secure" (Ecclus. 4:15). "Ecclesiasticus" means "the church's book" because it was esteemed by the early Christian church.

The Wisdom of Solomon was probably written somewhere between 100 BCE and 50 CE by an anonymous sage who adopted the name of King Solomon for the purposes of his book. This sounds rather like the situation of Ecclesiastes. But Wisdom of Solomon was written in Greek, probably by a Jew in Alexandria. Nevertheless, the work seems to be familiar with Ecclesiastes because, evidently, it criticizes him. The Wisdom of Solomon expounds on the justice of God and the use of wisdom as a guide for life. By chapter 2, the writer condemns the "ungodly" who say, "Short and sorrowful is our life, and there is no remedy when a life comes to its end." He does not mention Ecclesiastes, but scholars surmise that the writer had Ecclesiastes in mind when he ridicules and parodies the "seize the day" notion: " 'Let us take our fill of costly wine and perfumes, and let no flower of spring pass us by. Let us crown ourselves with rosebuds before they wither. Let none of us fail to share in our revelry; everywhere let us leave signs of enjoyment, because this is our portion, and this our lot. Let us oppress the righteous poor man" (The Wisdom of Solomon 2:7-10).[2]

Yet neither Ecclesiasticus nor The Wisdom of Solomon was included in the main canonical Bible. Ecclesiasticus was left out of the Hebrew Bible probably because his views of the afterlife displeased the ruling Pharisees. The Wisdom of Solomon, written in Greek, came too late; it was considered too recent to be part of the golden age of biblical works.

Ecclesiastes, against the odds, peers out at us from inside the sacred vessel that denied entry to his would-be counterparts and rivals.

> Alas for you, O land, when your king is a servant,
> and your princes feast in the morning!
> Happy are you, O land, when your king is a nobleman,
> and your princes feast at the proper time—
> for strength, and not for drunkenness!
> Through sloth the roof sinks in,
> and through indolence the house leaks.
> Feasts are made for laughter;
> wine gladdens life, and money meets every need.
> Do not curse the king, even in your thoughts,
> or curse the rich, even in your bedroom;
> for a bird of the air may carry your voice,
> or some winged creature tell the matter. (10:16-20)

What does the Bible say about government and political power? The matter is never far from Ecclesiastes' thoughts. He's preoccupied with the right relationship of kings to the nation, and passing along court etiquette to students.

Does God bless government? Is there a biblically correct form of government? Israel's early history was galvanized by the politics of tribal clans, but soon monarchy and empire ruled the day. Kingdoms were forces of unity. They protected borders. In the long political history covered by scripture, there's no talk of democracy, a much later development—no discussion of voting rights, pollsters, landslides and reelections, or the separation of church and state. Monarchy—either Israelite kings themselves, or antagonistic foreign rulers holding sway over Israelite society and later the Christian minority—was antiquity's only form of government.

By Ecclesiastes' time, Israel had been used to kings since the days of Saul, some seven hundred years before. But the nation was always ambivalent about kingship.[3] A question lurked in the background: If God is the real king, what's the point of a human monarch? Kings in Israel were never understood to be absolute dictators who were above the law. They had responsibilities to carry out God's purposes. Prophets stepped forward to criticize and resist the king if he sank into immoral excesses and lawlessness.[4] God alone was ruler.

So a theme of uneasiness about kings was there from the start. The discomfort only grew louder once Israel came under the domination of alien monarchs. That's the world in which Ecclesiastes wrote. This passage reflects his own ambivalence. He seems to take a swipe at kings who appear weak; he also counsels elaborate prudence and caution when talking about the king.

In the next two hundred years after Ecclesiastes, voices got bolder, more resistant. The Maccabean Revolt, in the second and first centuries BCE, was a Jewish war against Israel's foreign oppressor, the Greek-oriented Seleucid dynasty, based in Syria. "An undisciplined king ruins his people," says Ecclesiasticus (10:3), and, "The Lord overthrows the thrones of rulers, and enthrones the lowly in their place" (Ecclus. 10:14). Against this political backdrop, perhaps a century later, a hymn of praise was sung by a young girl named Mary, as scholar Ellen Davis notes.[5] In her Magnificat anticipating the birth of Jesus, Mary would help change the political world with words that reach back to biblical history and forward to a future of unimagined upheaval and redemption:

> His mercy is for those who fear him
> from generation to generation.
> He has shown strength with his arm;
> he has scattered the proud in the thoughts of their hearts.
> He has brought down the powerful from their thrones,
> and lifted up the lowly;
> he has filled the hungry with good things,
> and sent the rich away empty. (Luke 1:50-53)

To this day, the world is haunted by this connection of God and government. In the United States there's no talk of kings but all sorts of talk about righteous government and how should morality infuse secular politics and who should lead it. The issue marks a great divide. Some citizens insist the thread from biblical times to ours is unbroken: God alone grants government authority. (In

Romans 13:1, Paul writes, "Let every person be subject to the governing authorities; for there is no authority except from God, and those authorities that exist have been instituted by God.") So it's important that government stand for the right things, the right set of values.

But which values? Religious conservatives emphasize personal and family morality: government should help create a climate where absolute values of personal behavior are honored and strengthened. Religious liberals emphasize fairness and the Golden Rule: government exists to protect society's underdogs and promote social justice in the name of a healthy body politic, which would destroy itself otherwise through inequality, deregulation, and corruption.

Ecclesiastes may seem far from modern notions of religion and politics. But in choppy chapter 10, he never strays from the dream of finding a wise leader or from warning about the consequences of public folly and how quickly the former can slide into the latter.

CHAPTER 11

WHO KNOWS?

Send out your bread upon the waters,
for after many days you will get it back.
Divide your means seven ways, or even eight,
for you do not know what disaster may happen on earth.
—Ecclesiastes 11:1-2

The more I read Ecclesiastes, the more questions I'd like to ask him. What was his real name? Who were his parents? What was he like as a teenager? Did he have a family? What made him laugh? What was his favorite verse of scripture? Did he travel, and where? What was the craziest thing he ever did? Did he write his book by himself at one sitting, or did he go through many drafts? Was he a faithful worshiper? Did he feel the presence of God? What were his final thoughts and last words? Who came to his funeral? Where was he buried? Is Ecclesiastes in heaven?

In chapter 11, the questions continue. Ecclesiastes approaches a homecoming. His pace quickens. His time is nearly up. He has more to tell his young students before releasing them into the wide world. He regards them with affection. He worries about them, surely. So he prepares to send them off with last-minute advice for the road. His language is a curious mix—vivid images, full of practicality, yet not so easy to understand.

I trust the message was clear enough to his audiences. To me, less so. He seems to be offering business advice—be prudent; diversify; provide responsibly for your heirs; keep your affairs in order. Or is he pleading for everyone to be generous without overly worrying about the risk?

Some readers find Ecclesiastes an unsettling experience and blame him for being a fatalist, glum and hopeless. Whatever his exact meaning, Ecclesiastes shows himself here to be future-oriented, not fatalistic. Plan for the future, he says, even while knowing disaster could strike. Ecclesiastes sounds rather like a modern financial planner—or a homeland security chief. Ecclesiastes is no more fatalistic than a citizen of the twenty-first century. The contemporary obsession with big cars and indifference to oil conservation shows a reckless disregard for future generations. That looks like fatalism to me.

But that's where we live now, caught between two attitudes, conflicted all the way, caffeine fueling the daily ride. One is fatalistic worry about the likelihood of terrorism or financial collapse or epidemic or even asteroids (according to the most recent scarifying science hypothesis). The other is irrepressible optimism, which includes three beliefs: (1) Someday we'll all strike it rich; (2) technology will save the day and provide the world with cheap new energy sources; and (3) we'll win all the wars and remake a peaceful world. I hope they're right. Politicians can't talk too much about intractable social problems or future sacrifice. If they do, national pundits will label them the worst thing you can call an American—a pessimist. That's why they don't quote Ecclesiastes much either. They could start by turning to chapter 11.

When clouds are full, they empty rain on the earth;
whether a tree falls to the south or to the north,
in the place where the tree falls, there it will lie.
Whoever observes the wind will not sow;
and whoever regards the clouds will not reap.
Just as you do not know how the breath
comes to the bones in the mother's womb,

so you do not know the work of God, who makes everything.
In the morning sow your seed, and at evening do not let your
hands be idle; for you do not know which will prosper,
this or that, or whether both alike will be good. (11:3-6)

Saying things like this, Ecclesiastes will never be the most popular guy in the room. We cannot know "the work of God," he says. We can't know how things will turn out. Does he speak this with sadness? serenity? anger? Does he take perverse pleasure in sounding gloomy? Yet what he says is perfectly obvious. No one knows next week's weather or the hour of death. And what would we do with the information if we knew? The future is the unmapped country where we are constantly arriving.

But because of biblical faith, a force arrives to help people cope with this condition of floating blindly into the future—the Holy Spirit. Since the time of the Bible, this spirit has been felt or known as the sudden guiding power of God, inspiring and impelling individuals or groups "with qualities they would not otherwise possess."[1]

There is no reference to the Holy Spirit in the book of Ecclesiastes. I don't think Ecclesiastes should be faulted for failing to refer to the Holy Spirit of Christianity's holy Trinity. But he declines to consider a spiritual power that animates both the Hebrew Scriptures and the New Testament.

It's a lazy cliché to say the Old Testament God has a personality that's quite different from the New Testament God. Some people talk as if they are two different Gods, the "God of judgment" belonging to the Old Testament and the "God of mercy" infusing the New Testament. This misperception does violence to divine judgment *and* divine mercy, both of which are found in both testaments.

And so is the Holy Spirit. The Old Testament usually calls it the spirit of the Lord (only three times is it actually called holy spirit— Ps. 51:11; Isa. 63:10, 11). This Spirit gives Samson physical strength (Judg. 14:6), causes frenzies of ecstatic behavior (1 Sam. 10:6), and guides the major prophets, notably Ezekiel and Isaiah.[2] In the New Testament the Holy Spirit arrives in newly dramatic fashion. Jesus is identified as the eternal bearer of the Spirit. After the first Easter, the outpouring of the Holy Spirit on believers initiates a foundational moment for the emerging church, the new faith in the resurrected, ascended Jesus Christ.

Ecclesiastes urges awe of God and warns of God's judgment. But the Christian reader's biggest stumbling block with Ecclesiastes might always be the sage's lack of acknowledgment of the freedom and working of the Spirit. Nevertheless it is intriguing to note that the languages of the Bible have no distinct word for *spirit*. The English word *spirit* comes from the Latin word for breath, *spiritus*. In Hebrew the word means breath or wind.[3] Ecclesiastes was very aware of wind—its mysterious comings and goings, its symbolic power as a life force that blows in our faces but remains uncontrollable, unpredictable, invisible. It's both a gentle breeze and a category 5 hurricane. These are also properties of the Spirit. Jesus made an observation that could have been at home in the book of Ecclesiastes: "The wind blows where it chooses, and you hear the sound of it, but you do not know where it comes from or where it goes" (John 3:8). Then he added world-shattering words of destiny: "So it is with everyone who is born of the Spirit."

It is impossible to say how Ecclesiastes finally regarded the motions of the wind, the "spirit"—as a mere meteorological fact? a distinct sign of the unstoppable mysteries of God? Add those to the list of questions for him.

> Light is sweet, and it is pleasant for the eyes to see the sun. Even those who live many years should rejoice in them all; yet let them remember that the days of darkness will be many. All that comes is vanity. (11:7-8)

There are days when the sky is enough. It's enough to sit in a chair, look up, and stare.

Such days defined unhurried childhood—summer clouds, afternoon baseball scores, the sky's blue sweep reaching incredibly into deep space. No schedule, no wristwatch. Then, for the next thirty years of career bustle, no skyward gazing—no lazy looking up, just straight ahead, alert for the next bend, the next train to catch.

Not today, not this minute. I stare up, agreeing with Ecclesiastes that "light is sweet." It's enough to walk outside, hear birds in tall trees, and breathe. It's plenty to stare up at the silent extravagance overhead, the continuous big event called the sky. It waits, as if holding its breath. It's what we have in common with the ancients, this sky that drew their wildest guesses, their hardest questions about the meaning of it all. Ecclesiastes squinted into it. Jesus taught under it. In a few hours the night sky will deliver a different slate of biblical associations—Abraham scanning the stars in amazement at God's plan for his many descendants, and the wise men following the firmament to a fateful Judean nativity scene.

For now, no darkness, just light. The brooding big questions burn away in the sun. The heavy weather has passed, for now. Sweet light is the essence of this walking-around-and-good-to-be-alive life, the opposite of the grave, that dark, deep, below-ground physical destiny.

"The philosopher proves that the philosopher exists," poet Wallace Stevens said. "The poet merely enjoys existence." At such times everybody's a poet, sailing into balmy inner weather, far from rough seas, motion sickness, or the demand for perfectionist answers from ourselves. They're rare enough, these pleasant days "under the sun." How to savor and hang on to them? Ecclesiastes' answer keeps a cold arithmetic in mind—the days of darkness will be many. The play of light and dark—God made them both. Both are cornerstones of belief. Making peace with the light and the darkness somehow allows me to accept the present moment and harvest it, then move on to the next harvest and the next. These are the terms of God's creation, written in sky and soul, a theological treatise without words.

Recently we had to put our terminally ill cat to sleep. Ivan had an inoperable heart tumor. I took him outside one last time before heading miserably to the vet, just so he could enjoy once more what he loved, the sunlight. He hobbled around, took it in as he could. I'll always remember him in his prime under the bright sky, his gray tabby coat glistening, tail high, embracing his place in the sun for a while. The difference between us and Ivan, I suppose, is we know we will die. Gadgets and gossip are invented to divert people from the fact. When a culture denies death, the entertainment machines create fake substitutes for the darkness—movie violence, Internet fantasies, strip clubs, TV shows about glamorous hit men, death wishes big and small. They become a major sector of the economy. It's a strange business. Instead of biding our time in the light, people court the darkness, as if it cannot come soon enough.

But that's for another time. Today, the overpowering plenitude of the sky is enough.

> Rejoice, young man, while you are young, and let your heart cheer you in the days of your youth. Follow the inclination of your heart and the desire of your eyes, but know that for all these things God will bring you into judgment. Banish anxiety from your mind, and put away pain from your body; for youth and the dawn of life are vanity. (11:9-10)

When Ecclesiastes talks of God's judgment, I pay attention. He does this three times in his book. The first was at chapter 3, verse 17, where he says God will "judge the righteous and the wicked, for he has appointed a time for every matter, and for every work." We face the second reference now. It goes to the heart of what Ecclesiastes tells the world, if the world will hear it right. The third and final mention, in chapter 12, will be in the last passage of the book itself.

Ecclesiastes' talk of divine judgment changes my reading of him. Critics dismiss Ecclesiastes as a hopeless voice who concedes no relationship between God and people. Such critics will have to contend with these warnings about God's attentive judgment of people's lives. The biblical word *judgment* implies God is watching, a living connection between God and earth. Ecclesiastes, despite his reputation, embraces biblical tradition after all. If God is sovereign, then God is also ultimate judge of earth, all nations and individuals. Ecclesiastes does not dispute this concept, unless you are persuaded by scholars who argue that Ecclesiastes never wrote these words about divine judgment, that the passage was placed there later by a more orthodox editor.

What does Ecclesiastes mean by God's judgment? The Bible's idea is both emphatic and elusive. It goes back to Genesis 18:25, where Abraham said before the Lord, "Shall not the judge of all the earth do what is just?" It's found in the Psalms and the Prophets. In the Hebrew Scriptures, the judgment of God sometimes means the smashing of the wicked, or punishment of the Israelites for backsliding from God's laws, or, more positively, the eventual restoration of God's people. Either way, divine judgment is expected to take place in human history.[4] In the human story, the Author gets the last word on earth.

The book of Daniel takes a new turn, offering the Old Testament's only clear mention of individual resurrection, the prospect of judgment and redemption after death. Daniel 12:2-3 says, "Many of those who sleep in the dust of the earth shall awake, some to everlasting life, and some to shame and everlasting contempt. Those who are wise shall shine like the brightness of the sky, and those who lead many to righteousness, like the stars forever and forever." Likely this section of Daniel was written a century after Ecclesiastes, during an era of political persecution that shaped new thoughts about God's relationship with humanity.

In the New Testament the theme of God's judgment moves to the foreground. Jesus pointedly preached the coming day of judgment. He urged a revision of ethics, an intensification of love of God and neighbor, an expectation of the coming kingdom of God. The New Testament looks forward to God's ultimate judgment at the time of Jesus' Second Coming.

What Ecclesiastes meant in his time, meanwhile, is subject to dispute. Commentators come to opposite conclusions about his crucial phrase, "Follow the inclination of your heart and the desire of your eyes, but know that for all these things God will bring you into judgment."

It all comes down to that "but." The traditional interpretation says God looks with stern disapproval upon the sensual pursuits of heart and desire. Yet scholar Ellen Davis notes that the Hebrew can be translated as "and" or "but."[5] If we go with "and know that for all these things God will bring you into judgment," the meaning shifts. It appears Ecclesiastes is urging responsible behavior, but accountability to God includes following the inclinations of your heart, which God put there. Davis writes, "Our enjoyment is the right answer to God's abiding (it would not be wrong to say 'obsessive') interest in the creatures who bear something like a family resemblance to God. Is not the children's joy the answer that the parent's love most desires?"[6]

It may take time for wary readers to digest Ecclesiastes' vision of life. If we have a duty to be happy, it's because God put that sense of responsibility there for us to take up, no matter how fleeting this life is. This is an idea easily abused, easily misinterpreted as a license to excess. But that's no excuse to deny it's there or to refuse to tangle with it. Here is a moment of biblical generosity seldom acknowledged—a religious affirmation of the human desire for happiness. Robert Gordis, in his book *Koheleth the Man and His World: A Study of Ecclesiastes,* believes the duty to be happy is central to Ecclesiastes' message. As Gordis summarizes: "Koheleth's metaphysics postulates the existence of God, coupled with His creative power and limitless sovereignty. But beyond these attributes, Koheleth refuses to affirm anything about his God, except that He has revealed his will to his creatures by implanting in man an ineradicable desire for happiness. Koheleth's morality accordingly recognizes the pursuit of happiness as the goal. His religion is the combination of his theology and his ethics."[7]

Every passage of chapter 11 pits two opposing forces—the uncertainty of the future against the invitation, or demand, to receive the present moment and act on it. It's the divine gift. The future may be shaded by dread; shadows of catastrophe and judgment loom vaguely in the background. But the present is the only time there is—time for waking up or making preparations or making history or just taking note of the changing hues of day. In the Sermon on the Mount, Jesus said anxious worry is useless; no one ever gained life from it.

All is vanity indeed if no one takes up Ecclesiastes' offer to notice that the ever-changing light is sweet. "Rejoice, young man, while you are young," he famously says. None of us will ever be as young again as we are this moment.

CHAPTER 12

GOD ALONE

Remember your creator in the days of your youth, before the days
of trouble come, and the years draw near when you will say, "I
have no pleasure in them."

—Ecclesiastes 12:1

I was walking the grounds of a monastery during a visit on a cold
sunny day, when I saw two words chiseled into a stone wall: "God
Alone." The message was terse and unsentimental, a reminder, a
memorial, a sound bite from the ages. I stopped and stared.

"God Alone."

What does this phrase mean? It could mean many things. One
possibility: Worship only God. Don't be tempted to open the tent to
other deities—spiritual, material, or emotional. Glorify God alone.

Or it may mean God is alone. Only God is God. We are not
God. We pray for God's presence; we search for divine connection.
That longing defines the human world. But God is necessarily
alone, God being God. The hopes and prayers of faith say otherwise: heaven, or eternity, is where the creatures are privileged to
stand in God's glorified presence forever.

Or perhaps "God Alone" means, don't confuse God the Father
with Jesus the Son. Christians do this all the time—move back and
forth between God and Jesus sometimes as if there's no distinction

between them. Jesus is part of the divine Trinity, along with the Holy Spirit and God the Creator. They are three aspects, three personalities, of one God. Church tradition has always insisted on the unity of those three aspects—while also preserving distinctions among them. Jesus brought redemption, but he was sent by the Father. "God Alone" is a clarifying phrase, a reminder of the command of monotheism to worship only one God. Whenever that commandment fades into murkiness, a first principle of life erodes—gratitude to the Giver of life loses its edge and declines. So does criticism of human pretensions, the demand to be skeptical of every human bid to compete with God for power and credit.

"God Alone"—the words cast a shadow over Ecclesiastes' work. In his pre-Christian era, he speaks for a principle of affirmation and criticism, all at once. All is vanity, he says—except God alone. Embrace the moment—God alone provided it. Remember the oppressed, remember the dead—God alone is judge.

Ecclesiastes now adds another element: remember God in your youth. That's a lot to ask of a teenager or a twenty-something—the restless, overbooked, hopeful, despairing, energetic, overwhelmed, eager new generation. The youth brigade may be Ecclesiastes' stated audience, but I think he has another demographic in mind as well—anyone who has ever gotten older and watched his or her own youthfulness gradually evaporate in a haze. In other words, everybody.

Remember the Creator, he urges. Some of my favorite places involve two brute elements: stone and wind. Somehow those substances bring to mind the first hours of creation. Such a place of stone and wind may be a little church on the prairie, an old cemetery, a castle, or a battlefield—reality boiled down to basics of life and death.

Recently I visited Iona, the windswept historic little island off the western Scottish coast. Stone and wind were abundant. Iona has been a Celtic Christian outpost since 563 CE, when Saint Columba landed there from Ireland, started a church, and managed to Christianize much of Britain before he was done. After centuries of Viking invasion, long stretches of productive monastic work and prayer, then hostility and neglect under Reformation history, Iona is now a beacon of Celtic Christian revival, contemporary worship renewal, a vision of social justice and love of God's creation, a place of pilgrimage and growing theological influence. A visit will take you to one stone edifice after another—nunnery ruins eight hundred years old, a refurbished abbey and cloisters, the tall Celtic crosses that have stood at the spot for one thousand years.

The wind is a buffeting constant—Kansas with an ocean view. The wind and stone put you in touch with the rises and falls of history, the sheer wordless force of nature. Wind and stone in rugged settings overpower the distractions that separate us from elemental reality. At places like Iona, the distance is narrowed. In the city, daily comforts keep alive the fiction that we have control and power. Iona's pocked stone and wind strip away pretense. Ecclesiastes' wisdom tradition isn't terribly impressed by human cleverness. Wisdom views the rising sun and the majestic silences of nature as daily messages from God. God is patient; God waits for us to get it right—or continues to work with us, despite our every error and lapse of conscience, in the sinews of every prayer and doctrinal attempt, every compassionate act, every encounter with stone and wind, every effort to read scripture and remember the Creator.

Before the sun and the light and the moon and the stars are darkened and the clouds return with the rain; in the day when the guards of the house tremble, and the strong men are bent, and the women who grind cease working because they are few, and those who look through the windows see dimly; when the doors on the street are shut, and the sound of the grinding is low, and one rises up at the sound of a bird, and all the daughters of song are brought low; when one is afraid of heights, and terrors are in the road; the almond tree blossoms, the grasshopper drags itself along and desire fails; because all must go to their eternal home, and the mourners will go about the street; before the silver cord is snapped, and the golden bowl is broken, and the pitcher is broken at the fountain, and the wheel broken at the cistern, and the dust returns to the earth as it was, and the breath returns to God who gave it. Vanity of vanities, says the Teacher; all is vanity. (12:2-8)

I am reading Ecclesiastes' chapter 12 at 550 miles an hour, six miles above the earth, on a transatlantic flight. This is the power of religious tradition: a word from scripture shows up in the cracks, on the periphery of routine, in a carry-on bag, and adds something to the picture. It travels. It has legs. Ecclesiastes' great final poem, verses 2 through 8, is remarkable anywhere, but all the more so when it's read in unexpected places, like in a Boeing 757, row 27, during a night flight over the North Atlantic, with two hundred other earthlings packed in their seats, daydreaming, fidgeting, praying by the seat of their pants for another safe arrival.

We are hurtling—through air, through time, whether in a jet-liner at 550 miles per hour or sitting still in a chair—either way, racking up the miles, aging. Our culture does what it can to change the subject. The Botox posse is on twenty-four-hour call to keep alive the lucrative business of agelessness. The dolled-up models in the underwear commercials get younger and younger. Capitalism is in league with the god of eros: economic growth requires an unrelenting search for new markets, new images, new frontiers of titillation. There are no pop songs anymore about aging. Ecclesiastes has never been read, as far as I know, on MTV or the E! Channel.

But that doesn't stop him. Ecclesiastes hopes to grab young people by the shoulders while there's still time and help them see, touch, and taste the fragile beauty of their moment. He knows he does it in vain. Youth, they say, is wasted on the wrong people—a clever but meaningless line. Part of the pricelessness of youth is obliviousness to it. Teenagers wear the foolhardy, charming feeling of immortality. That's their job. Hearing such a poem as this won't be easy for them. Three decades removed from teenage nation, I'm all ears. I stand on a hill with a good view behind and ahead, standing somewhere in the middle, not quite (I hope) over the hill. There's nowhere to go but forward, no U-turns, and barely a turnout point for stopping for the view.

Traditional cultures honored their elders. The old folks were privileged because they were closest to the past, closest to the ancestors and holy stories. Such cultures had little social mobility, no aggressive youth culture or generation gap. The elderly were seen every day, part of the fabric of society. The entire community could internalize the insights of the aged and observe their decline and honor it.

The descent toward decay and ash—there's no use romanticizing it, and Ecclesiastes doesn't. He dignifies it without whitewashing it. Aging is tough sledding. There's a time to defy it, a time to accept it. I wake up every morning in defiance. But along the edges lately I've noticed something new, the possibility of accepting the unacceptable. The bones ache nearly every day. Someday the grip will slacken. There's less vitality to spend on all the endlessly recycled distractions that keep the culture spinning and talking about itself. Maybe the siphoning off of precious energy is what life is— all the horrendous wastes of time and money, the thrills, the mistakes, all the tears and folly. There used to be time to waste and still get work done. There's no time to waste anymore.

Ecclesiastes manages to express bitter experience without bitterness. This is his art. He invites us to share the vista where reconciliation meets mortality. This passage ranks up there with what he wrote in chapter 3. Commentators have outdone themselves analyzing this cascade of images of decline, trying to unlock their symbolic meanings. The passage reads like a valedictory statement, a last will and testament—his dying words? Some of the earliest scholars identified the images as anatomical symbols for decline of the aging body: the "guards of the house" are the knees, the "women who grind" are the teeth, the "doors" are the feet or the lips, the silenced "daughters of song" means deafness.[1] Leave off all the speculation, and the words still carry the reader. This passage is a river of poetry, a current rejecting rationalized analysis and arriving at its appointment with death. Ecclesiastes' eloquence offers readers an eternal moment of resistance. Remember God in your youth, says this master of paradox—and the rest of the time. For my last breath will return to God, where it finally belongs.

Besides being wise, the Teacher also taught the people knowledge, weighing and studying and arranging many proverbs. The Teacher sought to find pleasing words, and he wrote words of truth plainly. (12:9-10)

Suddenly the narrative shifts to third person, "the Teacher." Why? It's one of the mysteries of Ecclesiastes.

One explanation: Ecclesiastes, who was facing down death in the previous passage, died, and a friend stepped in to offer a brief eulogy, a summary of his life, an obituary that pays homage to Ecclesiastes' passion for teaching and his literary skill.

Another explanation: This is the moment in the narrative where an editor intervened and took over the rest of the book, in order to soften the blow of Ecclesiastes' unorthodox teaching by adding some warm religious feeling and making the point that Ecclesiastes was a wise and good man despite some careless words from time to time.

Yet another theory: Ecclesiastes himself used third person simply as a literary device to bring the book to a close. Perhaps all along, "Ecclesiastes" was a character that an anonymous writer invented to explore his own edgy ideas. In any case this theory implies only one author wrote the book of Ecclesiastes—one intriguing personality testing the limits of faith, one poet, one Ecclesiastes, not several.

"And he wrote words of truth plainly." Whoever Ecclesiastes' original audience was—young male elites? a more general populace?—the result was something new: a religious sage going against the religious grain in uncertain times, mixing philosophy and grievance, inspiring powerful opposition but prevailing in the end, winning a place in sacred scripture, connecting today with a world of individuals across twenty-three centuries. So how could he say there's nothing new under the sun? Doesn't his own work prove otherwise? The question nags Nobel Prize–winning Polish poet Wislawa Szymborska, who questioned Ecclesiastes directly in her Nobel acceptance speech in Stockholm in 1996:

> I bow very deeply before him, because he is one of the greatest poets, for me at least. Then I grab his hand. "There's nothing new under the sun": that's what you wrote, Ecclesiastes. But you yourself were born new under the sun. And the poem you created is also new under the sun, since no one wrote it down before you. And all your readers are also new under the sun,

since those who lived before you couldn't read your poem. And that cypress under which you're sitting hasn't been growing since the dawn of time. It came into being by way of another cypress similar to yours, but not exactly the same.

And Ecclesiastes, I'd also like to ask you what new thing under the sun you're planning to work on now? A further supplement to thoughts that you've already expressed? Or maybe you're tempted to contradict some of them now? . . . Have you taken notes yet, do you have drafts? I doubt that you'll say, "I've written everything down, I've got nothing left to add." There's no poet in the world who can say this, least of all a great poet like yourself.[2]

Ecclesiastes was something new. His presence in scripture was something new. So was the completion of the Bible itself. And, as long as we live, so is every new encounter with Ecclesiastes and the scripture that houses him.

The sayings of the wise are like goads, and like nails firmly fixed are the collected sayings that are given by one shepherd. Of anything beyond these, my child, beware. Of making many books there is no end, and much study is a weariness of the flesh. The end of the matter; all has been heard. (12:11-13a)

Gotcha, says Ecclesiastes to all us toiling writers of books.

Writing is endless and wearying, he says, so beware. Now he tells me! But we keep doing it. Why? Why has the Bible generated more books in the world than any other subject? The pull of its undertow is a mystery called the inspiration of the Bible.

The Bible speaks to us, for us, against us, despite us. It speaks. What does this mean? All the time as I was growing up, I heard scripture was inspired. The churches said so; the neighbors said so. The TV preachers did too, insisting on complicated theories of biblical infallibility. They left the impression that they'd rather defend the Bible than read it. Liberal believers gave a different impression. They largely withdrew from the debate about biblical authority, perhaps embarrassed by traditional talk of transcendence. They felt conflicted about whether or not the Bible is true and what truth means. This withdrawal and abdication created a public vacuum, a silence filled by fundamentalism's arguments and vocabulary, shaping the public's impression of faith, ethics, God, scripture, and people of faith for decades. This lopsidedness has been a tragedy for religion in America, alienating millions and distorting the historic faith. I've seen roomfuls of highly educated churchgoers get stuttery and tongue-tied the minute the discussion turns to biblical truth, biblical authority.

But when all the debating is done and it's time to open the Good Book itself, somehow the Bible generates a current between text and reader. It speaks from deep antiquity, arriving as a fearsome concoction of Holy Land history, miracle stories, human conflicts, and life-and-death news of redemption too compelling to ignore. Then we commence with commentary. Theoretically it is endless. The fixed and sanctified text meets the incessant flux of our daily circumstances, and the result must always be new combinations of impressions, questions, discoveries. Much study is a weariness of the flesh, Ecclesiastes warns. But he doesn't forbid it. He doesn't demand that we stop. Nor could he. In Judaism, study of scripture is the great dignified labor, incurring blessing. Christians inherited a reverence for scripture that goes back to the rabbi Jesus of Nazareth, who spoke with the deepest respect for the sacred texts of Israel, scrolls he took to be God-inspired. Ever since, "inspiration of the Bible" has meant that the Bible is dependable and truthful. No one has removed a word of it in two thousand years.

Nonetheless believers never agreed on exactly what *dependable* and *truthful* mean or how to articulate them. The early church fathers thought biblical truth meant absence of deception. Modern fundamentalism says biblical truth means absence of errors. To some, inspiration means the Bible is a literal divine oracle, words "breathed out" by God. A humanist argument says inspiration is simply the extraordinary importance that a reader happens to give these particular texts.

What does *inspired* mean? Christopher Bryan, a New Testament scholar and Anglican priest, says biblical inspiration should focus on the large purposes of the Bible. The purpose is salvation. The Bible is the vast witness to the story of salvation, the story through which God chooses to be known. The "inspiration" of the Bible is not to be seen as a thunderous moment when the text was hurled down from heaven or the day that everyone agreed these texts should be in the Holy Bible and others should not. Instead inspiration infuses the entire process, a process that continues in the reading and pondering of scripture to this very day. Says Bryan in *And God Spoke:*

> Inspiration is to be seen in the original experiences and vision that provoked the writers to write. It is in their calling to write, and their skills as writers. It is to be seen in the work of copyists and scribes, as well as in the discussions and thoughts of early theologians who determined that these texts were canonical. It is in the discussions and thoughts of theologians and exegetes ever since. Inspiration is at work in the work of modern translators and textual critics, and after they have done their work inspiration continues, right down to what goes on with you or me in that moment that we read or hear the Bible and are moved in response to attempt lives of faith and obedience, forgiving and forbearing one another as God for Christ's sake has forgiven us, clothing the naked, feeding the hungry, doing justice and loving mercy.[3]

As long as people experience the rattle and hum of the Bible and call it inspired, books about the Bible will always get written.

Fear God, and keep his commandments; for that is the whole duty of everyone. For God will bring every deed into judgment, including every secret thing, whether good or evil. (12:13b-14)

In the end Ecclesiastes wanders back home. He anchors his reckless thoughts, after all, in the history of the Bible—in the commandments and God's judgment. This passage gives readers a way to interpret everything else he says. It's the beam of light by which to read the rest of the book.

He skillfully withheld this passage until the end, sustaining suspense. We knew his book was a fierce exploration of the limits of faith. Now we know what his faith was in. His declaration, "Fear God," which he used several times before now, implied a loose framework of orthodoxy all along. How else to fear God except by keeping God's commandments? And which God did he mean? It's the God of Abraham and Jacob and Isaac and Sarah and Deborah and Jesus, or no God at all.

It's unfashionable nowadays to believe Ecclesiastes actually wrote these final words. They were added later, according to the guesses of many (not all) scholars. This theory says Ecclesiastes' heroic skeptical purity was tarnished at the end by pious orthodox fiddling, an editor's afterthought that (barely) achieved acceptance for Ecclesiastes in the biblical canon by making him look more religious than he really was. But it's a romanticized view of Ecclesiastes to say he believed in nothing, like a tortured dorm-room existentialist. "All is vanity" means life is fleeting, not life is meaningless. This poet, who never denied or escaped the God of scripture, found meaning in places his colleagues never imagined.

God will judge "every secret thing," he intriguingly says. I think of the secret life of faith and doubt, furtive emotions Ecclesiastes confronted in ways that organized religion customarily does not. Ecclesiastes comes to an end, but "the secret things"—the hidden treasures that motivate our lives for good or ill—carry forward. Even in the twenty-first century, the Bible itself is that treasure for untold numbers of believers, the only path of resistance to a billion falsehoods and indignities.

I like to think that an elusive master known as Ecclesiastes would agree.

ECCLESIASTES AND CHRIST

In a thousand ways, Jesus and Ecclesiastes diverge. Yet they are both in the same Bible. That's why I wrote this book.

The New Testament builds upon the Old. The good news in the New, the faith of Jesus and the faith in Jesus, gives us a new understanding of what God is like and what is possible in life.

But the Old Testament remains. The New Testament does not negate it, though some Christians are tempted to think so. Some condescend to the Hebrew Scriptures or quote selectively from them. Some are uneasy about the Hebrew Bible existing alongside the good news of Christ. But the New is not the death of the Old. They do not stand in fatal contradiction. Together they are the Bible. Together Old and New Testaments tell the story of God's search for humanity.

The church has always insisted on that unity. Jesus' attitude is the authority. Jesus quoted consistently from the Hebrew Scriptures—the Psalms, Genesis, Isaiah, Jonah. He considered the scriptures ordained by God. He said the "scripture cannot be annulled" (John 10:35).

Did Jesus quote from Ecclesiastes? There are intriguing parallels in the things they both said, but Jesus made no direct reference to him. It is plausible that the book of Ecclesiastes circulated in Jesus' time and caused a stir. But we don't know. Ecclesiastes was not securely in the Bible yet. It was accepted by some, rejected by others. The Jewish group Jesus knew best, the Pharisees, cleared the way for Ecclesiastes' inclusion in the holy book, but that didn't happen until several decades after Jesus' death and resurrection. Perhaps the scroll of Ecclesiastes came into Jesus' hands one day. If so, his reaction remains one of history's fascinating unknowns.

I said in the beginning that Ecclesiastes does not have the last word. He can only be, finally, a supplement to the faith you embrace. The book of Ecclesiastes cannot be the main story, nor does it ask to be. We all reach for a theological supplement of some sort to clarify our thinking, stir the mix, and move the faith forward. Some believers read Christian fiction or take long nature hikes or study Kabbalah or join a particular denomination with a particular history and interpretation of God and scripture. All are supplements to the story. This is how I read Ecclesiastes—framed by the rest of the Bible's vast campaign of commandments, injunctions, chronologies, miracles, and epiphanies. Ecclesiastes doesn't labor through those themes; many other books in scripture are there to do that necessary work. In that sense Ecclesiastes lives in the borrowed light of others.

But he's a conspicuous piece in the Bible puzzle. Ecclesiastes is a beaker filled with earthly elements—the passage of time, life's beauty and limitations, the divine silences, the consolations and confusions of our allotted days on earth, the poetry of the human condition. A few drops from Ecclesiastes' beaker into the well water of the faith are a healthy thing. Without them religion takes ungodly flight into realms of abstraction, pomposity, hysteria, and murderous purity. These prompt a person to claim too much— visions that turn out to be untrue, moral pronouncements that turn out to be mere bullying, divine errands that turn into bloodbaths. An old cycle gets revved up again—religious conflict, violence, disillusion, bewilderment, loss of faith, desecration, the name of God besmirched again and again, taken horribly in vain.

Ecclesiastes brings news from earth and keeps his feet on the ground, where real people face tomorrow and tomorrow. He wrote his words to honor all who've labored under the sun, the living and the dead, everyone who finds a blessing in the bright glint of the sunlight.

NOTES

CHAPTER 1

1. Paul J. Achtemeier, ed., *The HarperCollins Bible Dictionary* (San Francisco: HarperSanFrancisco, 1996), 167–68.
2. Geoffrey Wigoder, ed., *The New Encyclopedia of Judaism* (New York: New York University Press, 2002), 306–7.

CHAPTER 2

1. Achtemeier, *HarperCollins Bible Dictionary*, 258.
2. Robert Gordis, *Koheleth the Man and His World: A Study of Ecclesiastes* (New York: Schocken Books, 1968), 75.
3. Achtemeier, *HarperCollins Bible Dictionary*, 408.
4. Andrew Greeley, "The Puritans and American Politics" in *One Electorate under God? A Dialogue on Religion and American Politics,* eds. E. J. Dionne Jr., Jean Bethke Elshtain, and Kayla M. Drogosz (Washington, D.C.: Brookings Institution Press, 2004), 107.
5. Kevin Eckstrom, "Gallup Poll reveals growing number of Americans believe in heaven, hell," Religion News Service, June 11, 2004, http://www.baptist standard.com.

CHAPTER 3

1. Gordis, *Koheleth*, 123–24.
2. Achtemeier, *HarperCollins Bible Dictionary*, 866.
3. The Book of Common Prayer (New York: Oxford University Press, 1990), 265.

CHAPTER 4

1. David Noel Freedman, ed., *The Anchor Bible Dictionary* (New York: Doubleday, 1992), 5:402–14.
2. Beth Shulman, "Working and Poor in the USA," *The Nation* (February 9, 2004): 20–21.
3. Elsa Tamez, *When the Horizons Close: Rereading the Book of Ecclesiastes* (Maryknoll, N.Y.: Orbis Books, 2000), v.
4. Ibid., 145.
5. Ibid., 144.
6. Ellen F. Davis, *Proverbs, Ecclesiastes, and the Song of Songs* (Louisville, Ky.: Westminster John Knox Press, 2003), 189–91.
7. Robert Gnuse, "Inspiration of Scripture," in Walter Harrelson, ed., *The New Interpreter's Study Bible* (Nashville, Tenn.: Abingdon Press, 2003), 2258–59.
8. Kathleen Norris, *Amazing Grace: A Vocabulary of Faith* (New York: Riverhead Books, 1998), 277–78.

CHAPTER 5

1. *The New Oxford Annotated Bible,* ed. Bruce Metzger and Roland Murphy (New York: Oxford University Press, 1991), 841.
2. Annie Dillard, *The Writing Life* (New York: HarperTrade, 1990), 32–33.
3. Davis, *Proverbs, Ecclesiastes, and the Song of Songs,* 196.

CHAPTER 6

1. Alan Richardson, ed., *A Theological Word Book of the Bible* (New York: Macmillan, 1951), 108.

2. Ibid.
3. Achtemeier, *HarperCollins Bible Dictionary*, 381.

CHAPTER 7
1. *Gregory of Nyssa—Homilies on Ecclesiastes an English Version with Supporting Studies: Proceedings of the 7th International Colloquium on Gregory of Nyssa (St. Andrews, Sept. 5–10, 1990)*, ed. Stuart George Hall (Hawthorne, N.Y.: Walter de Gruyter, 1993), 32.
2. Ibid., 34.
3. Ibid., 98.
4. Davis, *Proverbs, Ecclesiastes, and the Song of Songs*, 201.
5. Norbert Lohfink, *Qoheleth: A Continental Commentary*, trans. Sean McEvenue (Minneapolis, Minn.: Fortress Press, 2003), 4–5.
6. Ibid., 6.
7. Davis, *Proverbs, Ecclesiastes, and the Song of Songs*, 205.

CHAPTER 8
1. Richard Elliott Friedman, *The Disappearance of God: A Divine Mystery* (Boston, Mass.: Little, Brown and Co., 1995), 83–84.
2. Lohfink, *Qoheleth*, 104.

CHAPTER 9
1. Achtemeier, *HarperCollins Bible Dictionary*, 891.
2. Alan Richardson, ed., *A Dictionary of Christian Theology* (Philadelphia, Pa.: Westminster Press, 1969), 159.
3. Phyllis Trible, "Authority of the Bible," in Walter Harrelson, *The New Interpreter's Study Bible*, 2251.

CHAPTER 10
1. C. L. Seow, "Ecclesiastes: A New Translation with Introduction and Commentary," *Anchor Bible* (New York: Doubleday, 1997), 21–36.
2. See note in Harrelson, *New Interpreter's Study Bible*, 1423.
3. Achtemeier, *HarperCollins Bible Dictionary*, 567.
4. Ibid.
5. Davis, *Proverbs, Ecclesiastes, and the Song of Songs*, 217.

CHAPTER 11
1. Achtemeier, *HarperCollins Bible Dictionary*, 432.
2. Bruce M. Metzger and Michael D. Coogan, eds., *The Oxford Companion to the Bible* (New York: Oxford University Press, 1993), 287.
3. Ibid.
4. Achtemeier, *HarperCollins Bible Dictionary*, 555.
5. Davis, *Proverbs, Ecclesiastes, and the Song of Songs*, 222.
6. Ibid., 223.
7. Gordis, *Koheleth*, 123.

CHAPTER 12
1. Gordis, *Koheleth*, 342–44.
2. Wislawa Szymborska, *Poems, New and Collected, 1957–1997*, trans. Stanislaw Baranczak and Clare Cavanagh (New York: Harcourt Brace, 1998), xv.
3. Christopher Bryan, *And God Spoke: The Authority of the Bible for the Church Today* (Cambridge, Mass.: Cowley Publications, 2002), 60–61.

ABOUT THE AUTHOR

Ray Waddle, a nationally known religion writer, has written on the subject of faith and society for more than two decades. He has been a lecturer on the adjunct faculty at Vanderbilt Divinity School, a retreat leader, and a columnist for *Interpreter* and *Presbyterian Voice* magazines. As religion editor for *The Tennessean* from 1984–2001, he won awards for his work and traveled on assignment across the United States and to Europe and Israel.

Born in Shreveport, Louisiana, Waddle earned a journalism degree from the University of Oklahoma and a master's degree in religious studies from Vanderbilt University. He is the author of *A Turbulent Peace: The Psalms for Our Times,* also published by Upper Room Books.